BEFORE YOU LEARN MUSIC THEORY

PRE-REQUISITE C

A REVOLUTIONARY WAY TO TEACH MUSIC THEORY

The Hat Publications

Copyrighted 2023

The pre-requisite course

What You Need to Know Before You Learn: Music Theory

Copyrighted 2023

Table of Contents:

Acknowledgments

Dedication

Preface

Introduction

SECTION 1- P.1

The Unifying Concept — P.1

Define- Music, Interplay, Consonance and Dissonance — P.1

Define-Context — P.2

Music Elements — P.3

Music Architecture — P.7

Construct and Compare 2 Compositions — P.8

SECTION 2- P.11

Principles of Sound — P.12

Musical Alphabet — P.17

If 12 Notes- Why 88 keys? — P.17

Musical Alphabet in Multiple Octaves — P.26

Why White and Raised Black Keys? — P.26

SECTION 3- P.29

Tonal Center — P.30

How and Why Consonance and Dissonance Is Created When Notes Interact-Intervals — P.30

SECTION 4- P.41

Intervals on a Sliding Scale of Consonance and Dissonance P.46

Create Any Interval Anywhere on the Piano P.49

Construct and Compare 2 Compositions P.53

SECTION 5- P.55

Use Intervals to Create and Understand Any Scale P.55

Create Any Scale, Using the Intervallic, Formula Anywhere on the Piano P.64

SECTION 6- P.70

Use Intervals and Scales, to Create Melody P.70

Rhythm- Metered vs Free Time P.82

SECTION 7- P.

What is Harmony, Harmonious, Harmonize and Harmony Section

Why Our Music Alphabet Uses Only 12 Notes, and Why These Specific 12?

What's Next

SECTION 8-

Music History- Evolution of Music Genres

Testimonials

Contact Us

Appendix

Author and Music Fractals

Acknowledgments:

To all my friends, teachers, and colleagues who have contributed their time, energy, and expertise to this project, Thank You. It was only with your help and guidance that this 'labor of love' came to fruition.

Dedication:

This book is dedicated to you, the student.

Preface:

The music theory and concepts in this pre-requisite course are taught via the piano but are applicable to all instruments. No piano, no problem- there are plenty of downloadable piano apps available to you.

This pre-requisite course is for:

- Anyone interested in becoming fluent in the language of music
- Anyone who wants an overview of how <u>all music is created and/or constructed</u>
- Anyone who wants to cultivate the skills needed to <u>play any song proficiently</u>
- Anyone who wants to cultivate the skills needed to <u>improvise and compose</u>
- For any player who has been or is being taught via one of the current learning methodologies, who doesn't fully grasp music theory- *who would like a music theory workbook*
- Anyone interested in a Music Appreciation Course
- For public or private music teachers who want a pre-requisite course, or a supplemental teaching guide to help reach their learning goals
- Kids-age 9 and above, adult beginners, intermediate players- *I suggest that kids 8 and under take the course with the help and guidance of a tutor*

How to Take This Pre-requisite Course:

For students who are interested in learning music theory, **please** read all the material and do all the suggested exercises-

- *The course takes approximately 8-12 sessions. However, this is just an estimation and it's best to move at your own pace*

- *I suggest 40-minute sessions- at least three times a week. Use the first 30 minutes to learn new material and then 10 minutes to review what you just learned*
- *On the second and subsequent days, I suggest using your first 5-10 minutes reviewing the previous lessons, followed by 25 minutes learning new material, and 10 minutes reviewing what you've learned*
- *I suggest printing out the images and charts from this course- allowing you to easily reference them throughout the course. The images and charts are free on our website,* www.beforeyoulearn.com

If you are a music teacher, use this course as a syllabus or supplemental teaching guide.

If you are a music student who is currently taking music lessons, use this course as a music theory workbook.

If you're a music appreciation student, take this course as if it were a documentary. *Read and listen to the videos without practicing.*

For everyone, read the History Section at your leisure.

Note: *Please understand that you are learning music theory and not how or what to play. This is meant to teach you the language of music and show you how others have communicated their ideas. During this course, some ideas and concepts will be more easily understood than others. If you're having trouble with one particular topic, read the next couple of pages; the explanation might be a page away. If the topic is still unclear, take a break. Give yourself time! Only move on to the next section when you are confident that you understand the material. A good way to judge if you know the material is to try to explain and demonstrate it to someone else.*

We are currently working on creating a student chat room for you to share your learning experience with other students. Please visit our website beforeyoulearn.com and subscribe- we will notify you when the chat room is completed.

Introduction:

We create and listen to music to satisfy our innate need to communicate or express what it means to be human- to share our stories, life lessons and evoke a range of feelings, moods, and emotions. Therefore, music is a language, and when learning any language, fluency is the goal.

Currently there are several teaching methodologies within the western tonal music system. Whether you agree with some over others, the general goal is the same—to teach the language of music. Unfortunately, current methods seem to be falling short. In fact, it is public knowledge that there is an unnecessarily high dropout rate, amongst other complaints. This issue is not only problematic for students but also has implications for teachers and society as a whole.

So, why are current teaching methodologies falling short?

In order to understand this, we need to look at the learning experience. The current teaching methodologies may be alienating because students do not fully comprehend why certain things work and others do not. Theory comes from the outside as something to simply accept. They, therefore, lack grammar or a narration that puts everything into context, making music theory accessible and meaningful.

Even though modern teaching methodologies have departed from the original "classical" method, which was designed to acquaint the student with music theory used by 17th-19th-century composers, they are continuously in a state of flux. Theory training now demands greater or lesser explanations of music before and after the classical era.

<u>This pre-requisite course aims to reframe the learning experience by adopting a remarkably simple yet astute assumption: all music, no matter the genre or time in history it was created, including all music theory terms and topics, can be distilled down to one Unifying Concept. This implies that understanding one concept is all you need to easily comprehend everything related to music. No matter what aspect of music you are discussing, it can be discussed in these terms.</u>

This new approach has proven to simplify the learning process; increasing the pace and ease at which students from around the world comprehend theory, saving time and money while reducing stress, confusion, and intimidation associated with learning. This is what differentiates this course from all other teaching methodologies.

We begin the course by stating the Unifying Concept- Music is the Interplay of Consonance and Dissonance.

Then, using a real-life metaphor, we define the terms Consonance, Dissonance, and Interplay, providing an easy language to aid student comprehension. From there, we slowly build a music example to illustrate the musical blueprint or the architecture used to create all music. We show how music is comprised of music elements that are assembled and varied like building blocks, whereas each variation will evoke a different feeling, mood, or emotion. *Which is the sole purpose of music.*

Furthermore, the student will learn that music can be made with any number of musical elements. You don't need to know all of them before you can start expressing yourself musically.

Learning music theory through this lens might seem deceptively simple, yet it offers several advantages. It is an innovative, fresh perspective that gives students an easily digestible, distilled overview of not only how music works but how everything in it is connected. Ultimately, it facilitates students with an empowering grammar that enables them to explore every new term or topic with confidence, culminating in a learning path that is not arduous but efficient and elegant.

SECTION 1—The Unifying Concept

All the music that has ever been made, or ever will be made, including all music theory terms and topics, can be distilled down to one Unifying Concept- **Music is the Interplay of Consonance and Dissonance**

Let's define these terms- Music, Interplay, Consonance, and Dissonance

Music can be defined as the result of organizing sound, in various ways, to express or communicate our story, to share life lessons, to evoke a range of feeling, moods, and emotions- *expressing what it means to be human.*

Interplay, Consonance and Dissonance are easier to understand through a relatable, 'real-life' example.

Imagine you're peacefully sitting at home, and you feel content. This is an example of **Consonance**.

After some arbitrary amount of time, you will naturally desire change. You're not going to want to sit at home indefinitely.

As the desire for change builds, tension (or restlessness) builds. This is an example of **Dissonance**.

As the tension mounts, you have a choice- *either let the pressure build, or release it*. Each choice, or each **Interplay**, will produce a different outcome.

Say, for example, you choose to release the tension and to do so, you go for a walk. That simple change is enough to release the tension and restore your sense of consonance. If you would have chosen to stay home, allowing the tension to continuously build, you would've eventually felt irritable, anxious or agitated.

It's the 'choices', or the **Interplay** between consonance and dissonance that will evoke the range of feelings, moods, and emotions that we experience in our everyday lives.

Music works in a similar way but we **'Interplay'** with Music Elements. We will explore music elements in the next section.

Note: *It's important to understand that nothing is perceived as consonant or dissonant until it is put into Context.*

Let me Explain-

Think of <u>Context</u> as the interrelated conditions in which something exists or occurs: environment, historical time frame, etc.…

Example-

- A cold-water pool in the hot desert **vs** a hot-water pool in the hot desert
- A cold-water pool in the arctic tundra **vs** a hot-water pool in the arctic tundra

It's the environment, or the <u>Context</u>, in which we experience the hot or cold water, that dictates if we perceive it as either consonant or dissonant *(e.g., if you were in a hot desert, a hot water pool would be perceived as dissonant whereas a cold-water pool would be refreshing and would be perceived as consonant).*

In our earlier example, 'sitting at home' was perceived as both consonant and dissonant- depending on the <u>Context</u>: 'sitting at home' was initially consonant, but as time passed tension grew and 'sitting at home' started to become less consonant and more dissonant.

<u>Therefore, nothing is definitively consonant or dissonant, rather consonance and dissonance are said to be fluid or on a sliding scale dependent upon Context.</u> Again, this is very important to comprehend and is applicable to everything in this pre-requisite course and onward. *This will become clearer as the course continues.*

Recap: Music is the Interplay of Consonance and Dissonance. Nothing is definitively consonant or dissonant, rather consonance and dissonance are said to be fluid or on a sliding scale dependent upon Context.

Note: *The terms-note, sound, tone, key, and frequency are synonyms. Throughout this course they will be used interchangeably*

Introduction to Music Elements:

Let's expand upon our real-life example of sitting at home to introduce and understand Music Elements. We will begin with 3 music elements but as the course progresses, we will explore others.

Note: You do not need to play the following examples. It is equally valuable to imagine how these examples would sound.

Imagine you're contently sitting in silence. This is an example of consonance.

As nice as 'sitting in silence' is, you're not going to want to 'sit in silence' indefinitely. After some arbitrary amount of time, you're naturally going to feel restless.

As the desire for change builds, tension builds. This is our example of consonance 'flowing' or 'sliding' towards dissonance.

But rather than an action (e.g., going for a walk) as a way to dissipate the tension, let's imagine playing a single note on your instrument.

The notes on your instrument are one example of a **Music Element.**

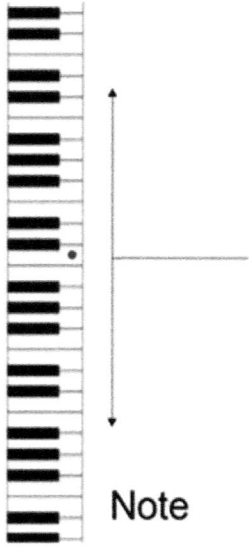

Think of the image on the page before as representing the range of notes you could choose to play. Here we see the slider is in the middle, representing the note in the middle of the keyboard. When you play that or any other single note, it effects a small change but it's enough to release the tension and restore your sense of consonance.

Now, imagine playing that one note, over and over. After some arbitrary amount of time, you will once again desire to introduce change. As this desire grows, tension builds.

So, what can you do? Well, you can introduce a change in **two** different ways.

You can either make a change to the Music Element (i.e., change the note you're playing) or you can add another Music Element.

Let's add another Musical Element-

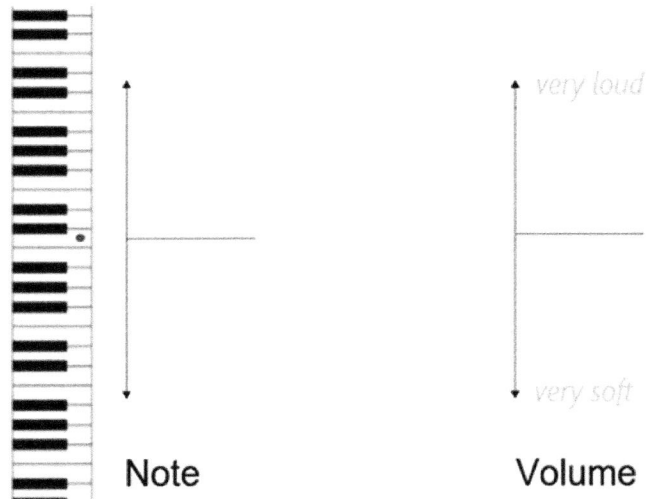

Note   Volume

Volume is another example of a Music Element.

Volume is how loud or soft a note is played. Just like the range of notes, volume is also a range. Here the second slider represents volume. The middle position of the slider represents an average volume, like our normal speaking volume (i.e., neither very loud, nor very soft).

So now you're going to play the same note, but you're going to make a change to the volume. *Image below*

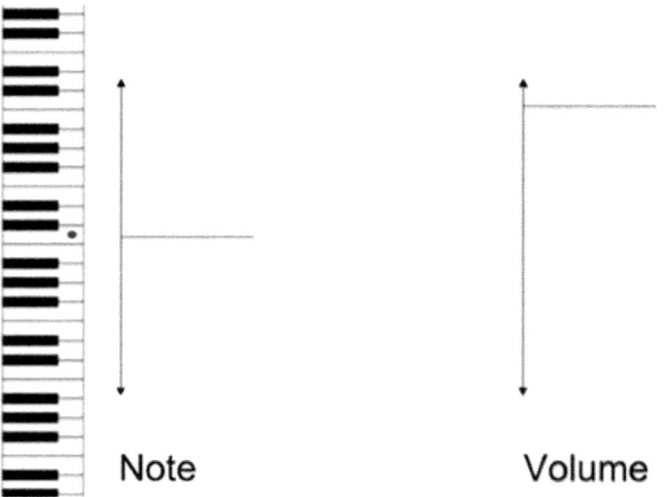

Again, it's a small change, but it's enough to release the tension and restore your sense of consonance.

Now, imagine playing the same note, with the same volume, over and over. I'm sure you're beginning to see the pattern: what was once consonant will 'slide' towards dissonance.

So, what can you do? Similarly, you can make a change to either of the Music Elements introduced so far (i.e., note or volume) or you can add another Music Element.

Let's add one last Music Element-

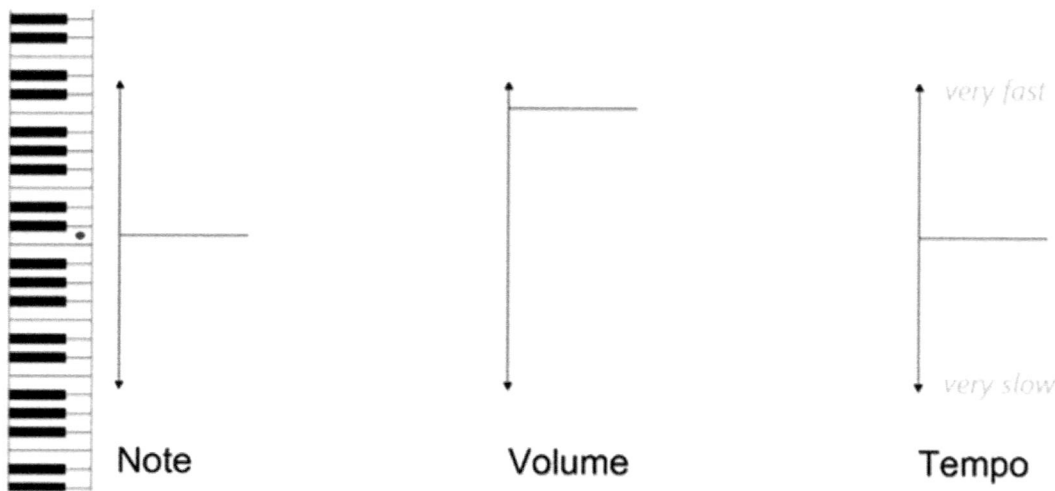

Tempo is another example of a Music Element.

Tempo is the pace at which the note is played. The third slider represents the range of tempos that you can choose to play. Above, we see the slider is in the middle, representing a commonly shared tempo (i.e., neither very fast, nor very slow).

So, imagine playing the same note, the same volume, but let's speed up the tempo. *Image below*

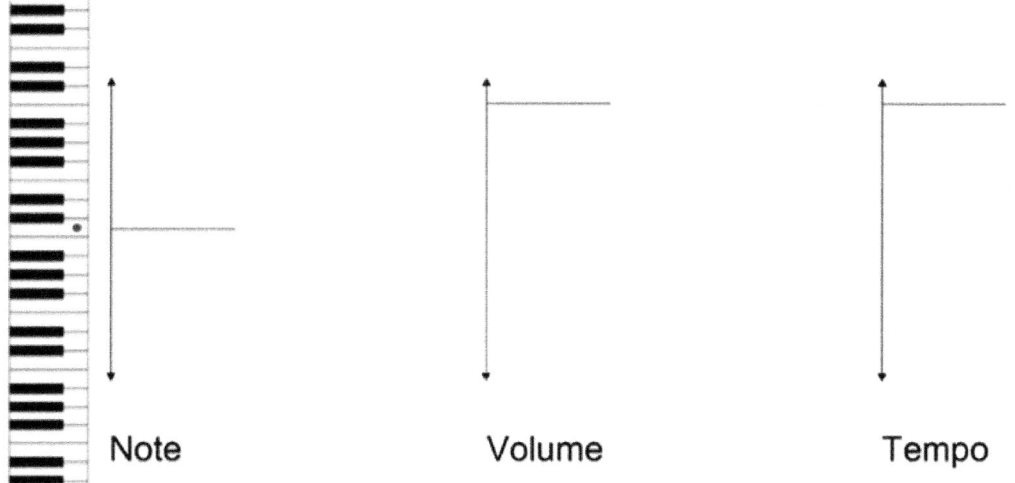

Again, you only introduced a small change but it can return the feeling of contentment- *at least for the moment.*

Note: *There are no formulas as to how much consonance or dissonance music or life should have, but one thing is for sure-if there was no interplay music and life would be monotonous.*

Great work!

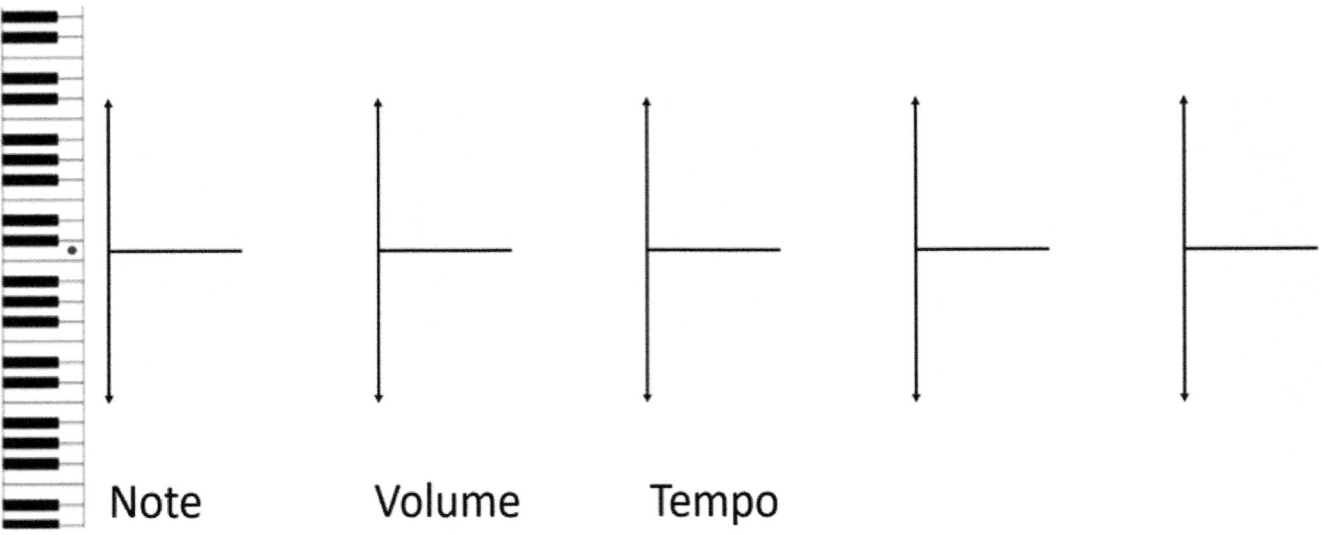

What this simple diagram shows us is the basic structure, the overview of how all music is constructed or composed! *(The two blank sliders represent music elements you will learn.)*

This is the Architecture of all music.

This diagram clearly shows us that all music is the Interplay of Consonance and Dissonance. That is, all music is simply layers of musical elements, whereas each element has a range of choices for us to interplay with. Each interplay, depending on Context, will be perceived as some level of consonance or dissonance; evoking a different feeling, mood, or emotion. *Which is sole purpose of music*

This is the blueprint that all musicians and composers use to create every style or genre of music you have ever heard, or ever will hear. From the healing sounds of Tibetan Singing Bowls, that use a minimal number of music elements, to the world record breaking symphony that was scored for 370 instruments and 106 vocalists.

Let's use the musical blueprint to construct two very simple compositions and compare- *You do not need to play the following examples. It is equally valuable to imagine how these examples would sound.*

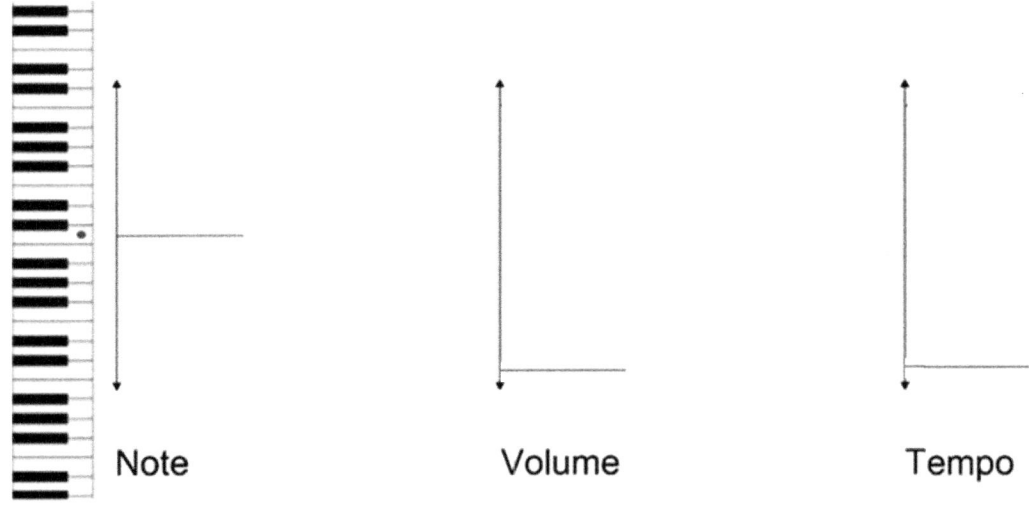

Vs.

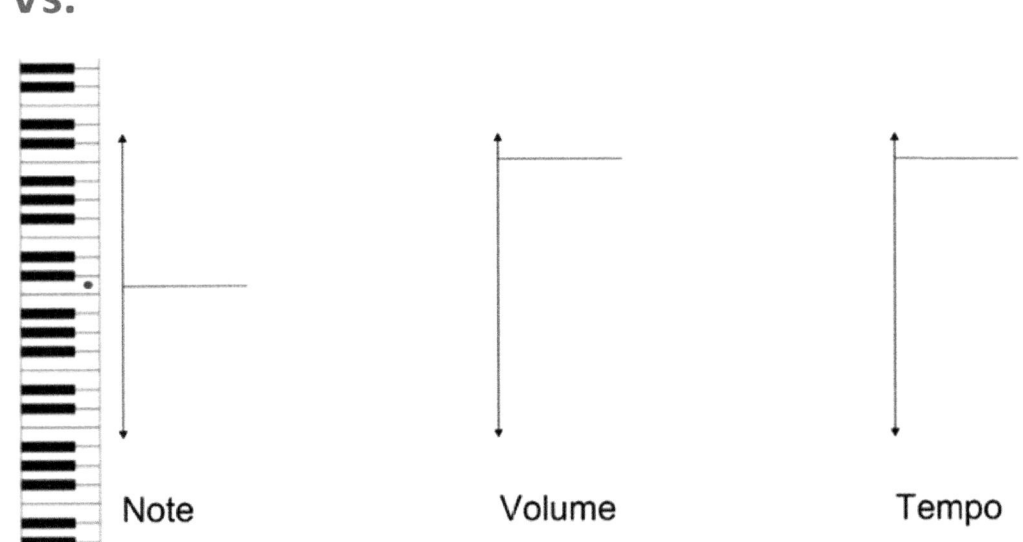

We see that both compositions are going to use the <u>same note.</u>

- The first composition has a very low volume and a very slow tempo.
- The second composition has a very high volume and an extremely fast tempo.

It should be clear that we would get two completely different outcomes. They are different for one reason and one reason alone- Music is the Interplay of Consonance and Dissonance.

Both of our two compositions "interplay" with the music elements differently; therefore, each evokes a different feeling, mood, or emotion.

Questions-

- Which composition would you choose to fall asleep to?
- Which composition would you choose to invigorate your energy?

Do you see that both compositions could be perceived as either consonant or dissonant depending on the Context?

-If you were trying to relax, the first composition would be perceived as consonant.

-If you wanted to be energized, the first composition would be perceived as dissonant.

And vice versa.

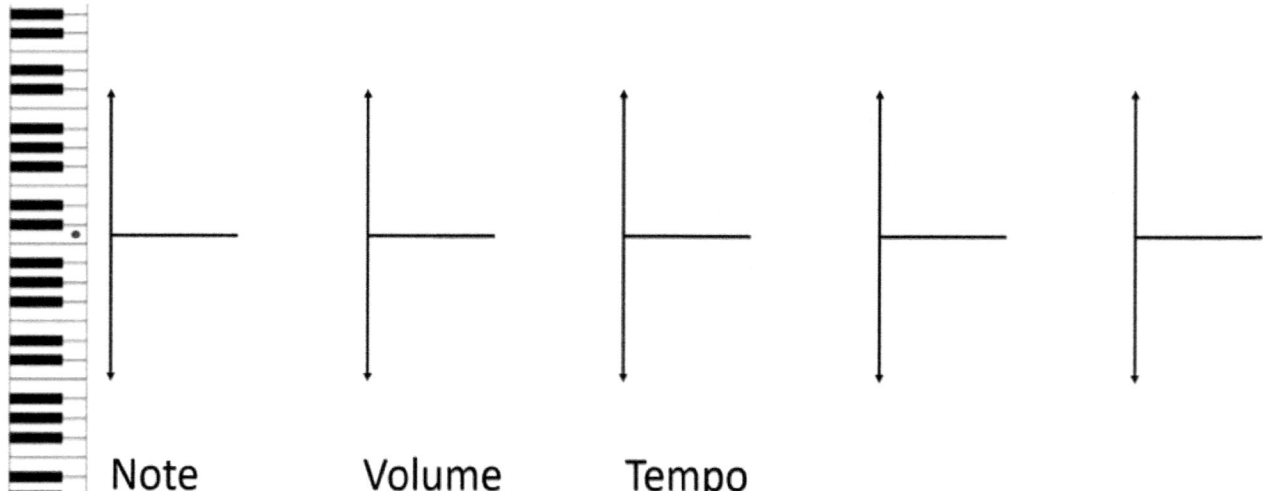

Note   Volume   Tempo

So far, we have only discussed three music elements, but of course there are many more. You might have heard of other music elements like rhythm, melody or scales. If you haven't, don't worry, as we will be covering them shortly. But for now, let's recognize that music can be made with *any* number of music elements. You don't need to learn all the music elements before you can start expressing yourself musically!

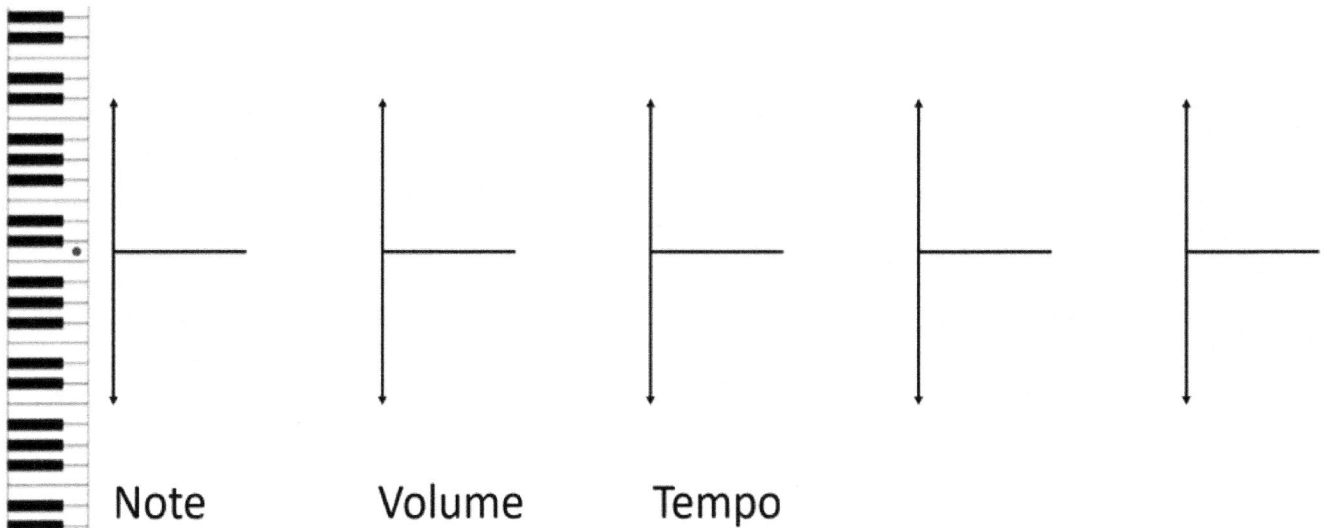

Another thing that this diagram shows us is that any music theory term that you encounter will generally only be one of two things- it will either describe a music element or instruct you how to play the music element.

Example-

- Volume is a music element: all the terms pertaining to volume will simply describe how softly or loudly to play
- Tempo is a music element: all the terms pertaining to tempo will simply describe how fast or slow to play

Now, you can approach any new term or topic with confidence by simply asking, "Is it a Music Element or is it describing how to play a Music Element?"

Great work!

Please*, review this section and make sure that everything is clear before you continue.*

Introduction to SECTION 2:

Since we don't need to know all the music elements before we can start expressing ourselves musically, we don't need to learn all of them in this pre-requisite course; however, it is *vital* to understand how any music element that has multiple notes interacting, like intervals, scales, and melodies, works. *We will be covering these shortly.*

When multiple notes interact, for example, when multiple instruments are playing together, or multiple people are singing together, the interacting notes are blending and/or mixing together. Each blend or mixture will not only sound different, but each mixture will be perceived as some level of consonance or dissonance; each evoking a different feeling, mood, or emotion. In order to understand "how and why?" each mixture evokes a different feeling, mood, or emotion, we first need to understand some basic **Principles of Sound**.

SECTION 2-

Basic Principles of Sound:

Let's listen to, and compare three music examples of notes interacting or mixing:

Music Example can be found here: https://beforeyoulearn.com/images-and-videos or

https://youtu.be/lBMv8j5jw1A

All 3 examples will have 2 notes interacting, blending, or mixing. The first note will always be the same, the second note will always be different. *Each example will play twice before moving on to the next. Please, give the video a few seconds to upload.*

As you listen, try to answer these questions:

- Which example, or examples, would you say sounded consonant?
- Which example, or examples, would you say sounded dissonant?
- Did each example evoke a different feeling, mood, or emotion?
- Can you put them in order, or on a sliding scale, from consonant to dissonant?

Please make a note of your answers as we will be revisiting them later.

Again, in order to understand how? and why? each mixture evoked a different feeling, mood, or emotion- we first need to understand some basic **Principles of Sound-**

Let's define these terms- *Soundwaves, Frequency, Music Alphabet, Frequency Multiples, and Octaves*

Whatever instrument you are playing, whether you are plucking a guitar string, blowing into a horn, or singing, the instrument is causing the air around you to vibrate, and it is this vibrating air that travels to your ears in waves.

These are called **Soundwaves**.

Every soundwave has its own unique measurement or **Frequency**.

Frequency, is simply the measurement of how fast a soundwave is vibrating.

- The slower the soundwave is vibrating, the lower the frequency.
- The faster the soundwave is vibrating, the higher the frequency.

Note: Every soundwave that has a different frequency is heard as a different sound.

Please, using your index finger from your right hand, **play** the furthest note on the left side of the piano. Now, **please play** the furthest note on the right side of the piano.

Which of the two notes sounded like the slower vibration, or the lower frequency?

Correct!

The furthest note on the left of the piano was the lower frequency. In fact, it is the lowest frequency on the piano. As you move from left to the right, the frequencies get progressively higher because the soundwaves are vibrating progressively faster.

Again, using your pointer finger from your right hand, start from the left, and working your way right **play** random notes- as you play listen as the frequencies vibrate progressively faster from left to right.

Note: In all the music examples you will be asked to play with either your pointer finger from your left or right hand. It's probably hard to believe that using only one finger will actually speed up your learning process. You won't be using any energy trying to figure what fingers to use.

How Frequency is Measured:

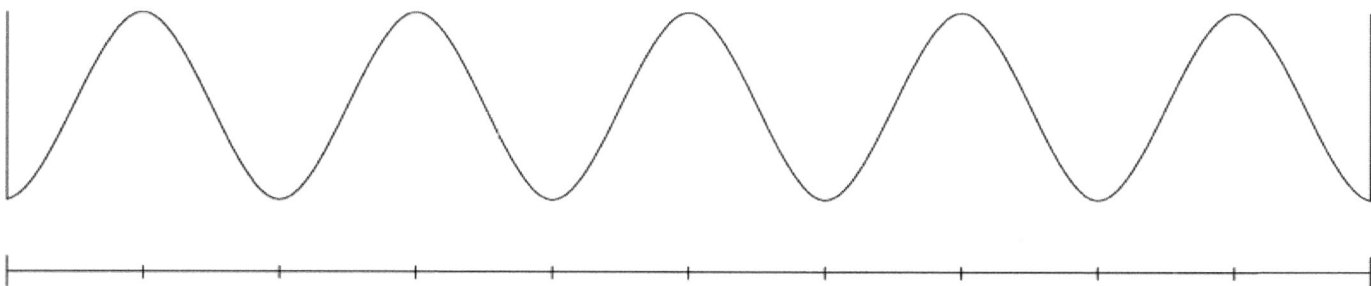

Instead of measuring the whole soundwave…

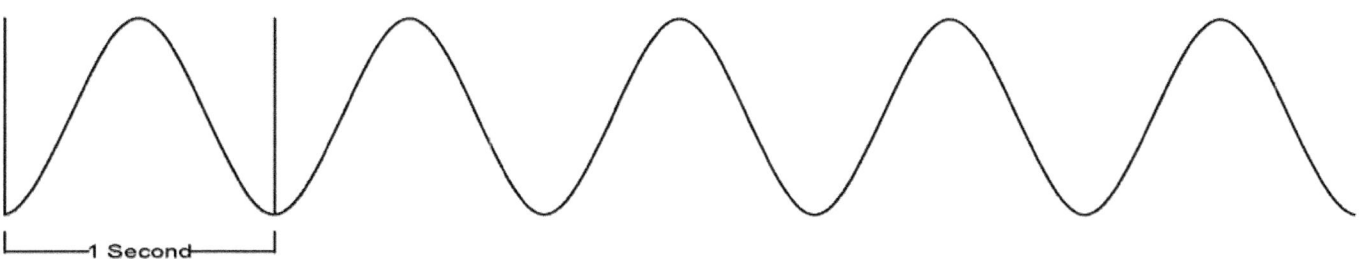

we can take a one second snap-shot of it, and then count how many waves pass a *given point* in that one second.

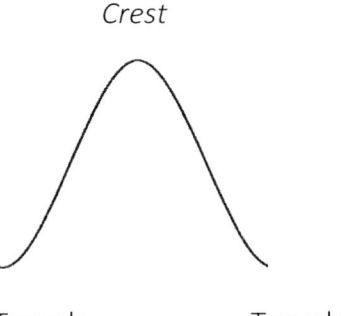

A wave is when one cycle of <u>Trough- Crest -Trough</u> is complete.

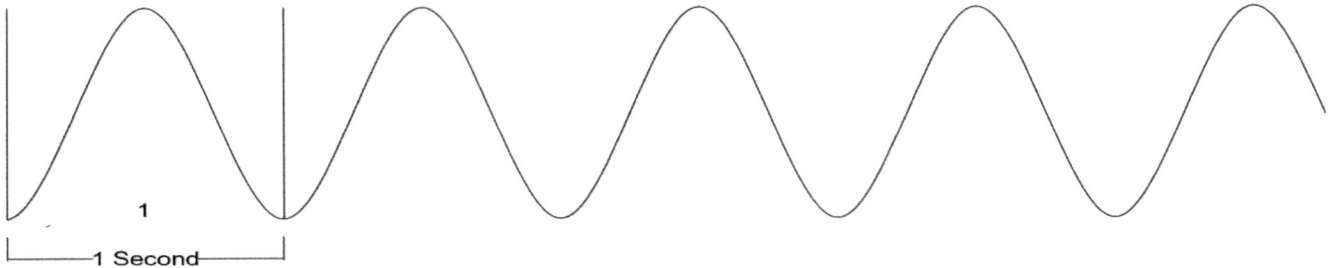

Example-

When we look at the above snapshot, we see that in one second 1 complete wave passed by...

So, this soundwave has a Frequency of 1.

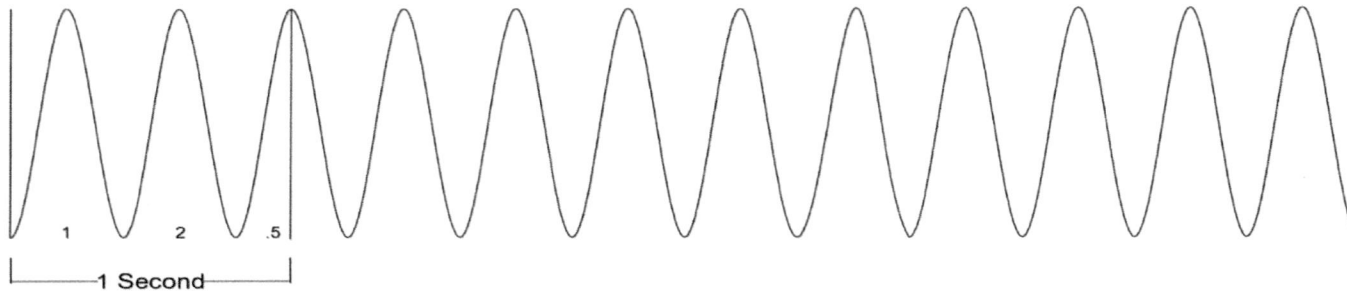

Example-

When we look at this snapshot, we see that in one second, two and a half waves passed by. That is, in one second two wave cycles have completed but even though the third wave has passed the given point at its crest, it is still not yet complete. It is only half of a wave cycle. So, this soundwave has a Frequency of 2.5.

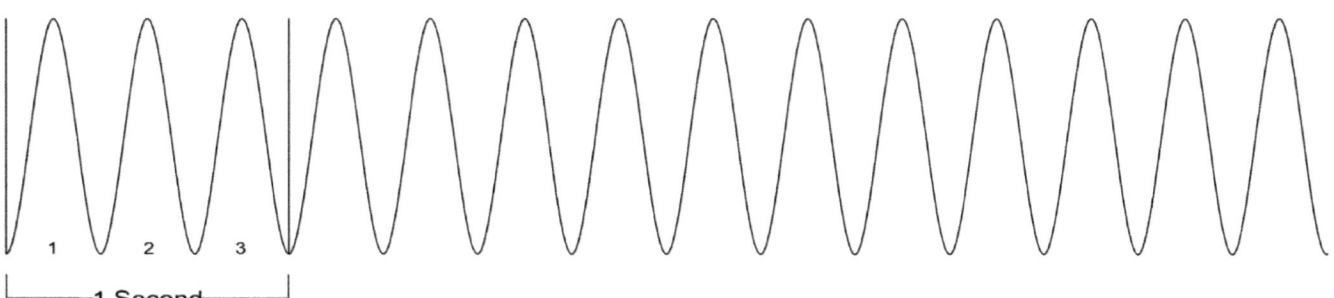

Example-

When we look at the above snapshot, we see that in one second, three waves have passed by. So, this soundwave has a Frequency of 3.

Great work!

Fun Fact:

There are an infinite number of frequencies in our universe!

If this is hard to comprehend, try to think of it this way:

- A soundwave could have a frequency of 3
- A soundwave could have a frequency of 3.1
- A soundwave could have a frequency of 3.11
- A soundwave could have a frequency of 3.111…

We can continue making new frequencies by simply adding another decimal place ad infinitum.

Thought provoking question-

If there is an infinite number of frequencies in our universe, why would our 'music alphabet' use only 12? Why these specific 12? Unlike the English alphabet of 26 letters, the 'music alphabet' only has 12 named frequencies- the names are not important at this time. We will be able to answer these questions by the end of this course. The answers will most likely surprise you!

The 12 Frequencies of our 'Music Alphabet'-

Below are the first 12 piano keys starting from the left side of piano. 27.5 is the first frequency of the Musical Alphabet. Don't worry, you don't need to memorize all these frequencies; we just need them to help us understand the concepts in this and upcoming sections.

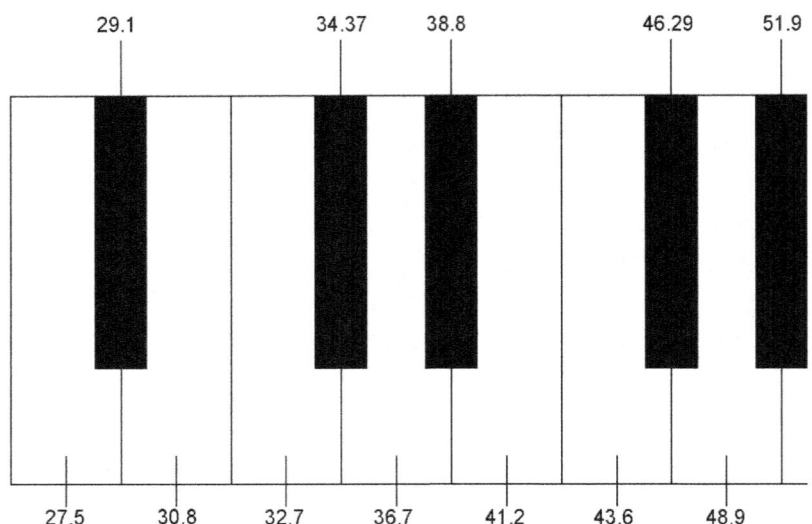

Note: These frequencies might seem more complicated than frequencies we have seen in our earlier examples. Please don't be intimidated! Just remember that every frequency is simply the measurement of how many waves pass a given point in one second. As the frequencies increase, the soundwaves are vibrating faster. Believe it or not, the first frequency on the piano (27.5) is almost the lowest frequency that humans can hear. Humans have the ability to hear frequencies that range from 20 all the way to 20,000. That's a big range but dogs can hear up to a frequency of 65,000!

Please, using your index finger from your right hand, **play** the 12 frequencies of the music alphabet in order starting from 27.5. (27.5 is the furthest piano key on the left side of the piano.)

If you listen closely, you will hear the frequencies vibrating faster as you move to the right.

Thought provoking question-

If there are 12 frequencies in our music alphabet, why would a piano, and all instruments for that matter, have more? Some pianos have less than 88 keys and some have more. The largest piano ever made has 108 keys!

Let me Explain-

Earlier we said, every soundwave that has a different frequency is heard as a different sound...

However, there is one exception-

When any frequency is doubled, we hear it as both different and similar at the same time. I agree, this is hard to comprehend but it will make sense in a moment and it will help us understand why most pianos have 88 keys.

Example-

If a soundwave with the frequency of 2 is <u>doubled</u>, we would have a soundwave with the frequency of 4. And if the frequency of 4 is <u>doubled,</u> we would have a frequency of 8...

The frequencies 2- 4- and 8 are in fact different frequencies, and even though we hear them as different sounds, they are also 'related' to each other. Since they are 'related' we also hear them as similar. We are able to hear both their difference and their similarity at the same time.

Let's take a look and see how they are related-

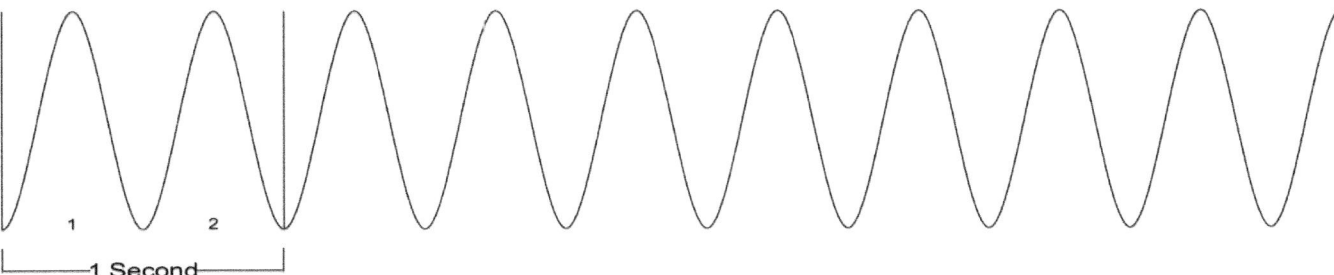

When we look at this snapshot, we see that in one second-two waves have passed by.

So, this soundwave has a frequency of 2.

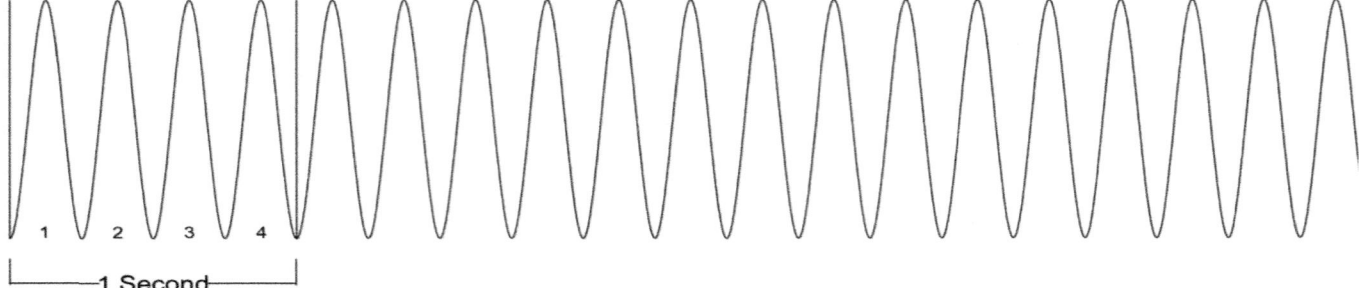

If we look at this snap shot, we see that in one second four waves have passed by.

So, this soundwave has a frequency of 4.

But we could perceive this snap shot in another way-

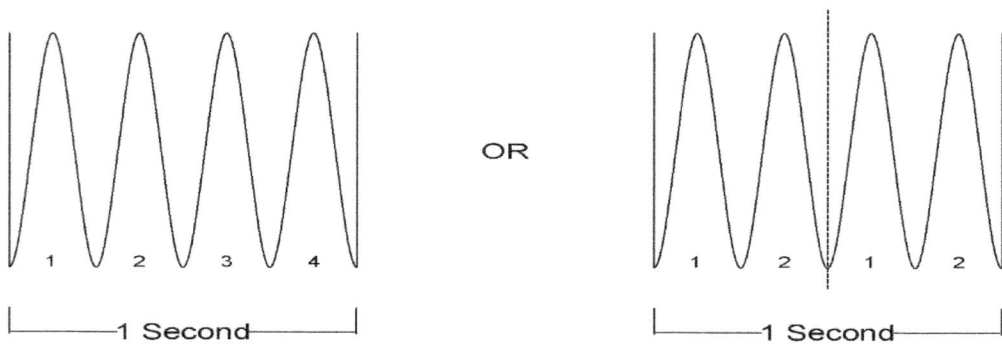

We can perceive it as either the frequency of 4, or as two sets of the frequency of 2.

It is the shared 'relation', to the frequency of 2, that allows us to hear them as similar.

For clarity, let's look at another Example- In the example below, we will use the frequency of the first note on the piano 27.5.

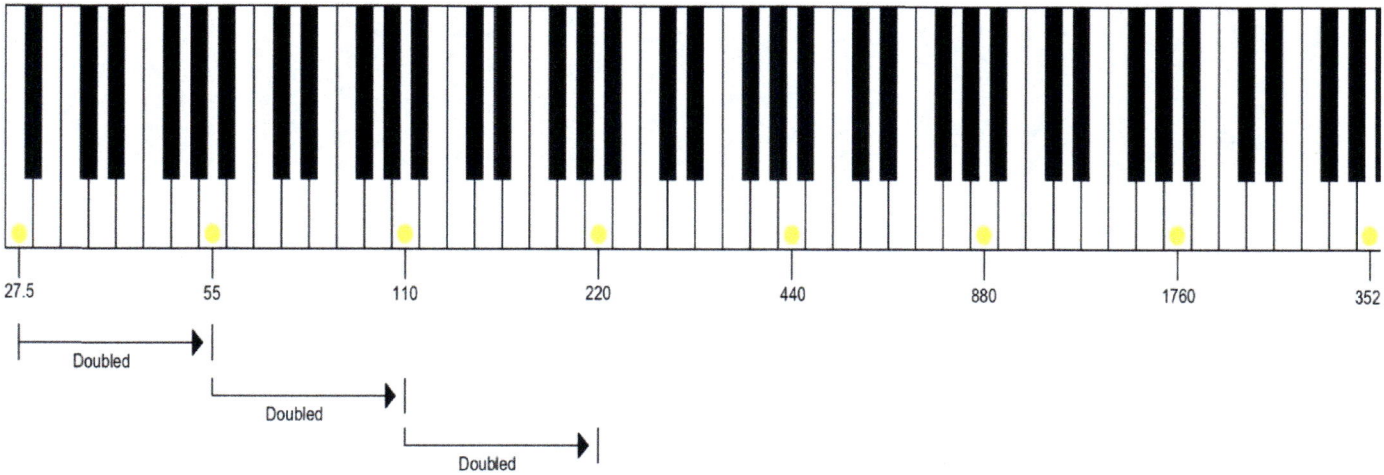

If we double the frequency 27.5, we would get a frequency of 55. If we doubled the frequency of 55, we would get 110 and so on.

27.5, 55, and 110 are in fact different frequencies and we do hear them as different sounds, but these frequencies are also 'related' to each other. Since they are 'related' we also hear them as similar.

Please, using the index finger on your right hand, **play** all the yellow dots starting on 27.5. Use the above diagram to help guide you. Take your time to locate each note and play the sequence a couple of times.

Do you hear the difference and the similarity?

Isn't that amazing?

Now, for comparison, start on 27.5 and **play** all the frequencies again, but this time instead of playing the yellow dot on 440, play the grey dot instead.

Question: Did the grey dot sound similar, or did it sound foreign?

Correct!

When you played the grey dot, it did not sound similar because the grey dot is not related.

Note: *If we can double a frequency, and recognize it as similar, then the opposite must be true. We can divide a frequency in half and recognize it as both different and similar.*

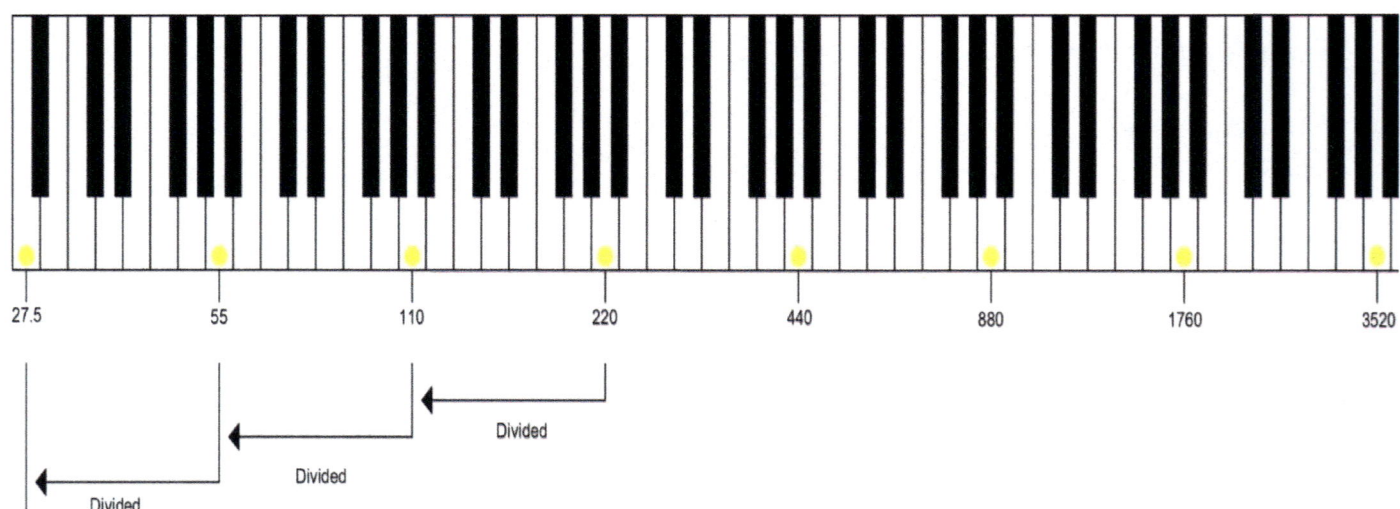

Example-

220 divided in half is 110 and 110 divided in half is 55 and 55 divided in half is 27.5.

Using the example from the previous page, use your index finger on your left hand, **start** on 3520 and **play** the all the yellow dots, from right to left.

Do you hear the difference and similarity?

Excellent!

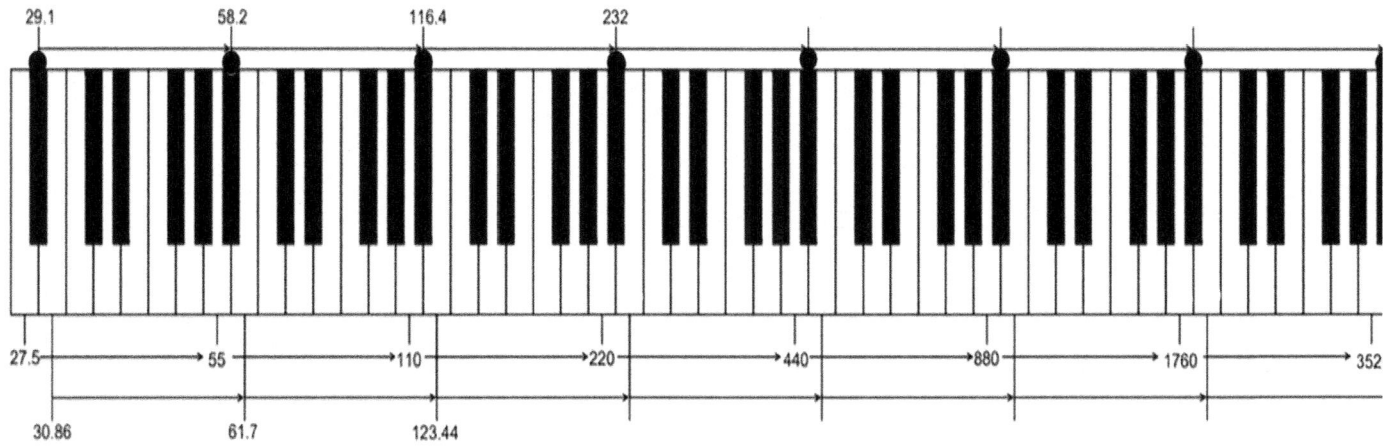

So, starting with 27.5, if we continued to double the 12 frequencies of the music alphabet, as many times as the piano will allow...

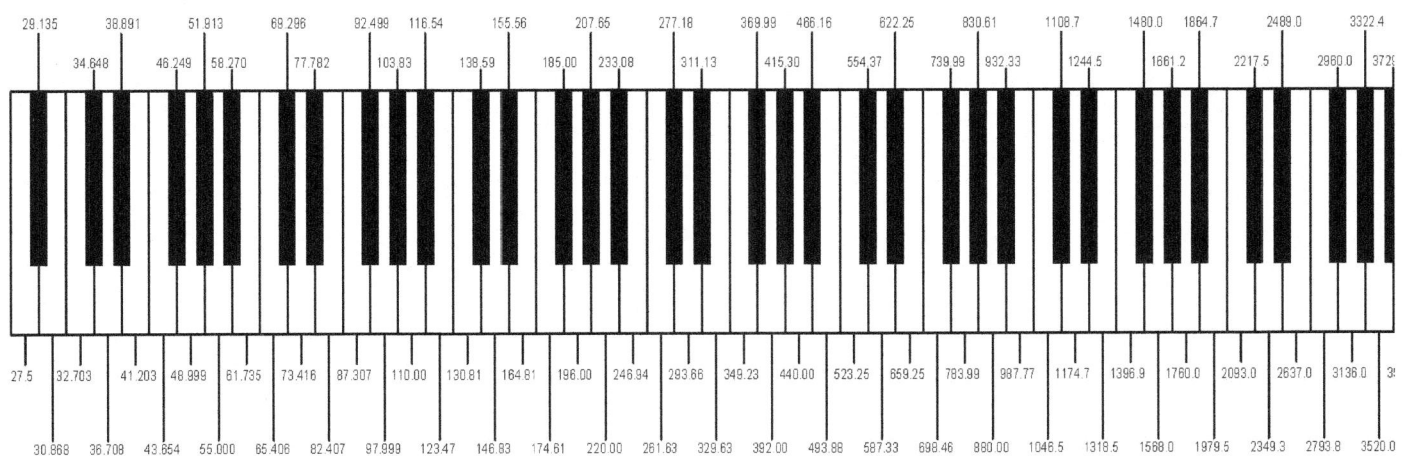

we will get all 88 frequencies! Don't worry, you don't need to memorize all these frequencies. It's just important that you understand where the frequencies on the piano come from.

It should be clear that all frequencies of the 'music alphabet' repeat in a cycle of 12 notes…

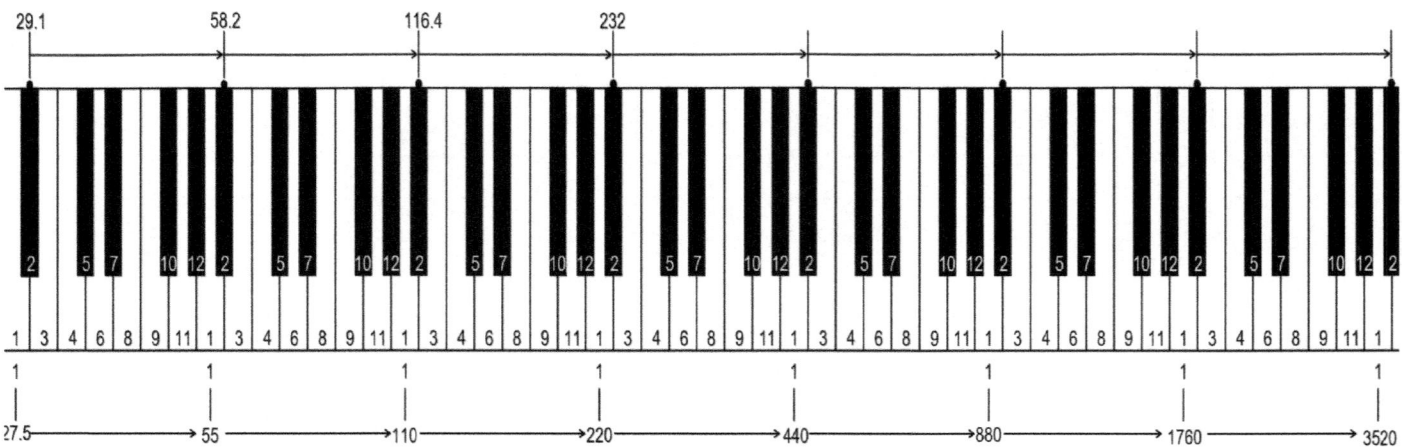

and that every time the music alphabet repeats, all the frequencies of the musical alphabet are doubled. Providing us with a variety of ways to play the music alphabet.

Please, using the pointer finger from your right hand, **play** the 12 frequencies of the music alphabet starting on 55. Now, for comparison **play** the 12 frequencies of the music alphabet starting on 220 then 880.

Do you hear the difference and similarity?

Isn't that amazing?

Note: Each repetition of the music alphabet is referred to as an 'Octave'.

Let me Explain

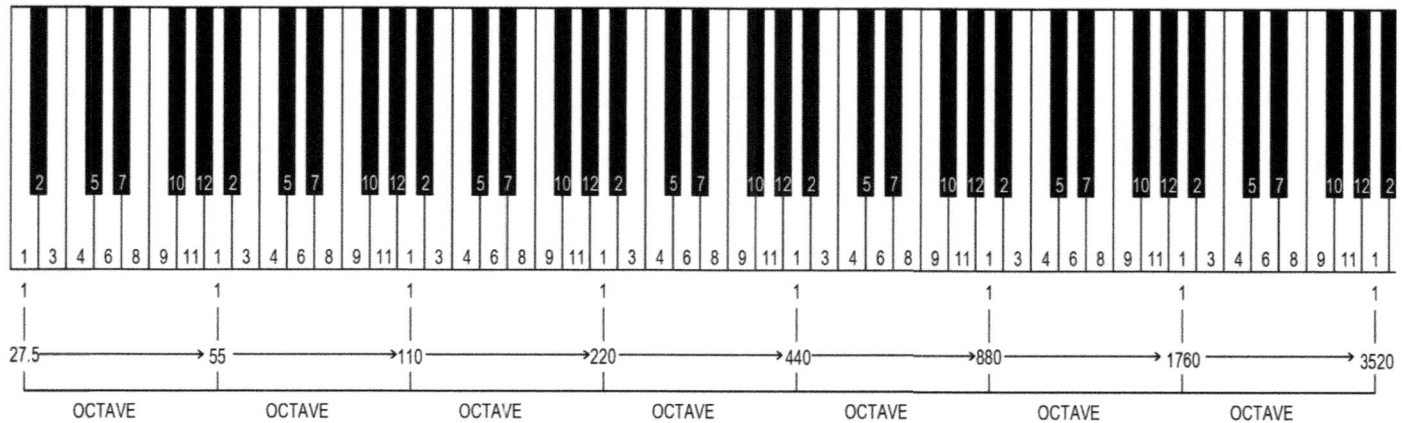

Octave is the musical term used to describe the 'distance' or the **'Interval'** of any two notes that are 12 notes apart.

Example- 27.5 and 55 are a distance of 12 notes apart, or an **Interval** of an **Octave** apart.

Since, within each octave, all the notes of the music alphabet are present, we refer to the frequencies of the music alphabet as being 'within an octave'. When we double all the frequencies of the music alphabet, the music alphabet is said to be an 'octave higher'. So, the term 'octave' can be referring to the distance of any two notes that are 12 notes apart, or referring to the group of notes that are within the distance of 12 notes (i.e., the music alphabet).

Furthermore, and this is admittedly confusing, the music alphabet can start on any note. No matter what note you start on when you count up 12 notes, or an octave, every note of the music alphabet will be included.

Example-

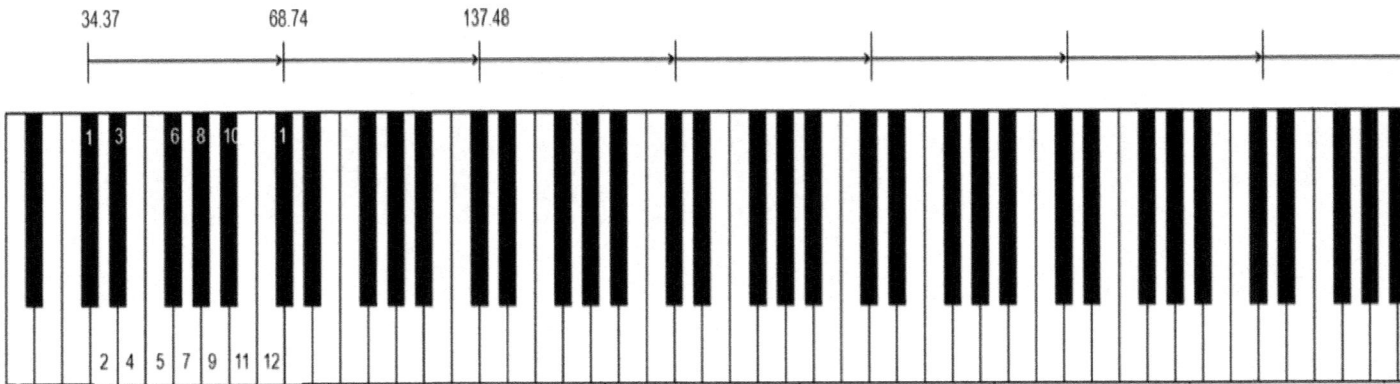

If we start the musical alphabet on 34.37, 68.74 is an octave higher- (above image). Within this octave, all 12 notes of the music alphabet are present, they are just in a different order due to starting on a different note.

Thought provoking question-

If all music was made using only the notes from one octave, what do you think would happen?

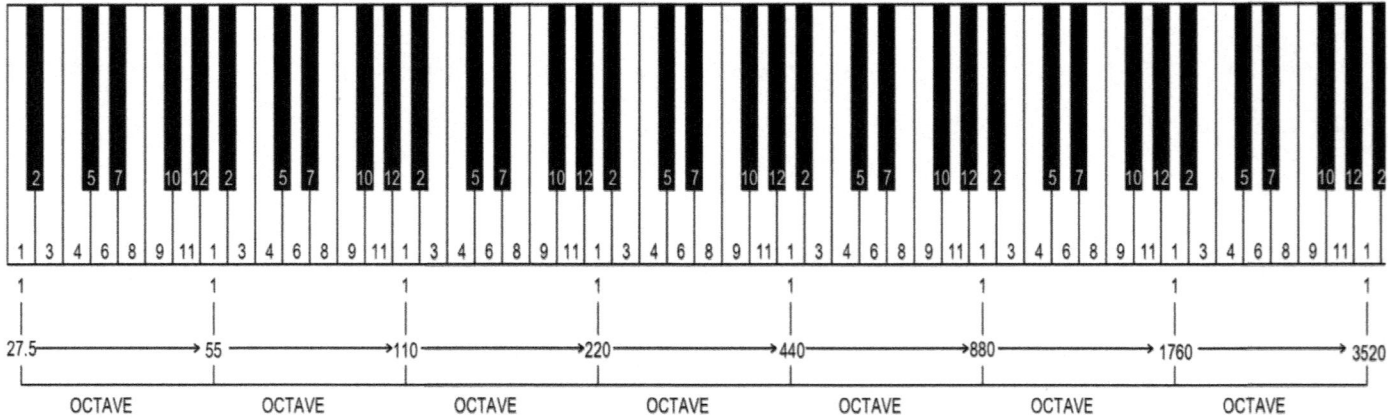

Please, using your pointer finger from your left hand, **play** some random notes using the frequencies from the first octave (i.e., the first 12 notes from the left side of the piano). While playing, imagine what it would be like if every song ever made (including those songs yet to be made) only used those notes.

Correct!

If all music was made only using the notes from one octave, music itself would become dissonant. You're already thinking like a musician.

Octaves are a Music Element:

Remember, we create music to express or communicate our story, our moods, our emotions, and what is meaningful to us. If we thought of each octave as representing, for example, a singer's voice then we can think of each octave as representing a different type of singer. The lower octaves would represent a deep voice (referred to as a bass), the higher octaves would represent a high voice (referred to as a soprano) and the middle octaves represent the average vocal range (referred to as alto and tenor). So, like every other music element that provides us with a range, <u>Octaves provide us with a range, or a variety, of ways to play the music alphabet.</u> We will compose and compare two music examples in an upcoming section.

Excellent work!

Bonus: Why are some piano keys black and some white?

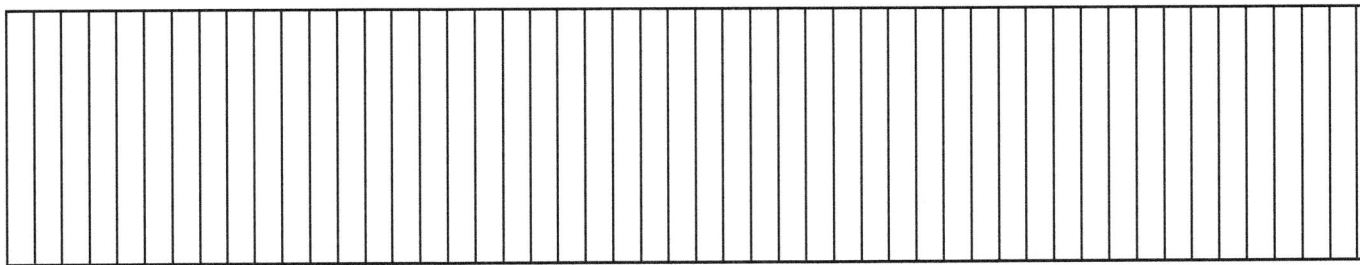

As you can see, it would be extremely difficult to locate the notes on a one-dimensional, all-white keyboard. The designers of the piano needed a functioning keyboard that allowed piano players to <u>quickly and efficiently</u> navigate their way around it, so they gave us 'landmarks'. With a combination of white keys and raised black keys, we can easily find the same note in any Octave. *The raised keys function like the bumps in Braille.*

Example-

If you wanted to play any note an octave higher, you could either count up 12 notes or you could use the 'landmarks' (the combination of white keys and raised black keys) to guide you.

For this example, let's use the yellow dot but any note will do.

If we make a quick observation, we see that the black keys are in groups of 2's and 3's except for the first black key on the left.

The 'yellow dot' is the white key to the left of the group of 2 black keys. If you wanted to play the 'yellow dot' an octave higher, you don't need to count up 12 notes one by one- instead simply look for the landmarks! The 'yellow dot' will always be the white key that is to the left of the group of 2 black keys!

Please, using your pointer finger from your right hand, **play** the yellow dots from left to right. As you play them, take notice of how the landmarks are always the same. In every octave the 'yellow dot' is always the white key to the left of the group of 2 black keys.

Now, **please** pick any 'new starting note', establish a landmark. Then using the landmark find the 'new starting note' in each octave.

Example-

The yellow dot is my 'new starting note'. I see that it is the first black key in the group of two black keys. Using this information, I can easily locate it in each octave. In every octave, the 'yellow dot' is always the first black key of the group of two black keys.

Please try this using at least 3 "new starting notes".

Being able to quickly and efficiently navigate the piano is incredibly beneficial to your playing. You will learn songs faster and use less effort.

Excellent Work!

Please, review this section before you continue and make sure everything is clear.

SECTION 3-

Let's listen again to the three music examples, and using the Principles of Sound lets answer these questions

Music Example can be found here: https://beforeyoulearn.com/images-and-videos or https://youtu.be/lBMv8j5jw1A

Remember, all 3 examples have 2 notes interacting. The first note is always the same, and the second note is always different.

Each example will play twice before moving on to the next. Please give the video a few seconds to upload.

- Which example or examples did you think were consonant?
- Which example or examples did you think were dissonant?
- Did you think each example evoked a different feeling mood, or emotion?
- What was the order of consonance to dissonance on your sliding scale?

I hope you agree that the first example sounded consonant, the second example sounded a little less consonant, and the third example sounded dissonant.

Furthermore, I hope you agree that each example evoked a different feeling, mood, or emotion. **Let's try and understand how and why.**

Hint- Nothing is perceived as consonant or dissonant until it is put into, and heard in, Context.

What we need to understand is that when any song starts, or in this case when a music example starts, the Initial sound is the environment, or the 'Context', in which we experience every sound that follows.

This means that the second sound is not heard in isolation, but rather is heard in relation to the Initial sound. This is the Context in which we experience the second sound. This dictates if we perceive it as either consonant or dissonant.

Or, in other words, the frequency of the second sound 'mixes' with the frequency of the Initial sound and like any mixture some will blend well and some mixtures will not.

We will look at our three music examples and analyze them in detail to make this clear.

Note: Since the Initial Sound is the Context for every sound that follows, it is referred to as the Tonal Center. Think of the word Tonal as another word for Initial sound, and think of Center as another word for Context. So, Tonal Center is another way of saying The Initial Sound is the Context in which we experience every sound that follows. For the rest of this course Tonal Center and Initial Sound will be used interchangeably.

But why do some mixtures blend well and others clash?
Let's take a look at our three examples and see how and why?

We identified the first 'mixture' you heard as consonant.

The frequency of the Initial sound used for every example (i.e., the Tonal Center) is 261. Marked below by the yellow dot.

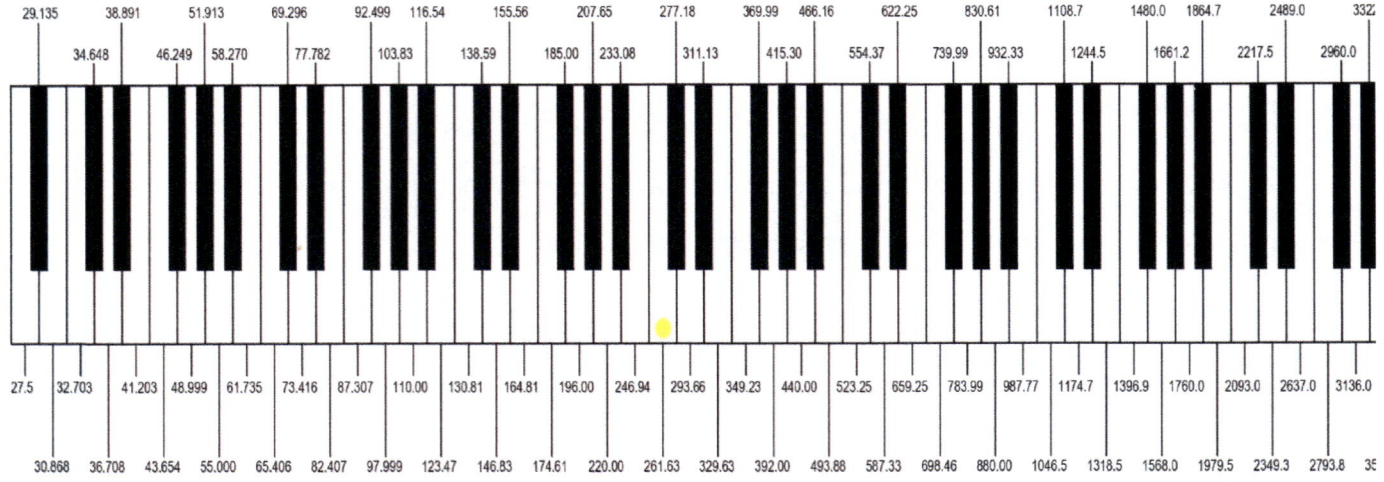

The frequency of the second sound was also 261. Marked by the grey dot in the image below.

Yes, you are right! I simply repeated the Initial sound. *But it is important to understand that, even though the sound waves were heard separately, the two soundwaves are still mixing together.*

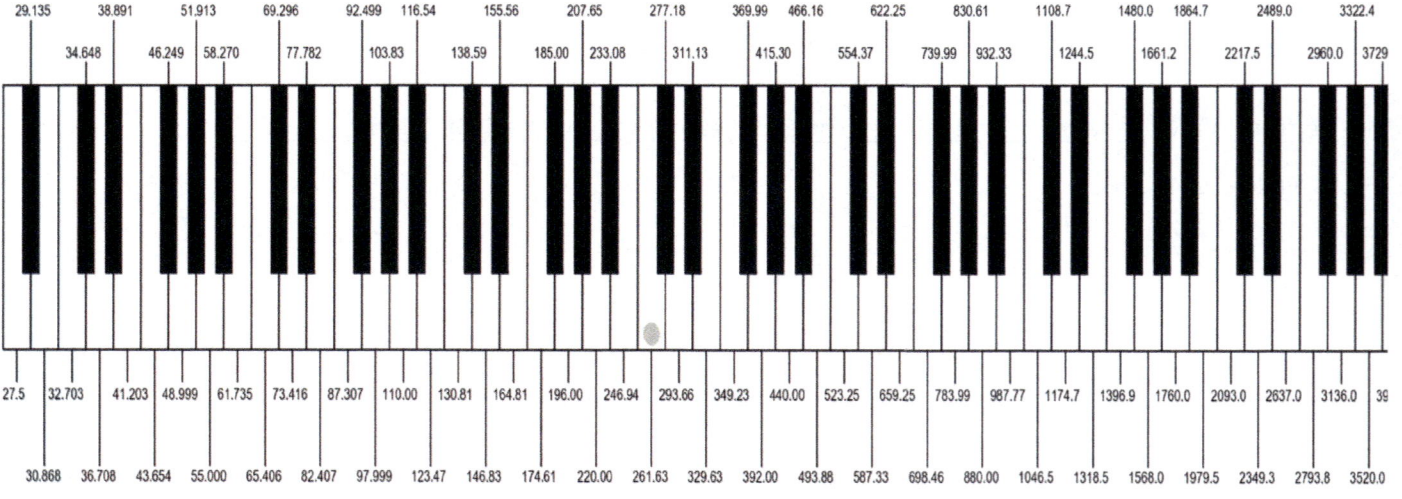

Please, using the index finger from your right hand, **play** the yellow dot, and then using the index finger from your left hand, **play** the grey dot.

The mixture of these two frequencies was heard as consonant because the two frequencies mix and/or merge together perfectly (like pouring milk into milk).

Here's a visual depiction-

The image below represents a section, or a 'detail' of the entire soundwave. It would be very difficult to see 261 waves in one second.

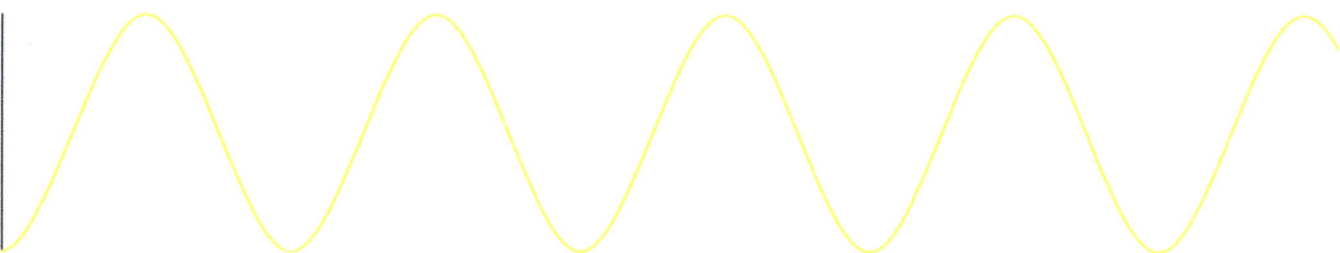

The Initial Soundwave.

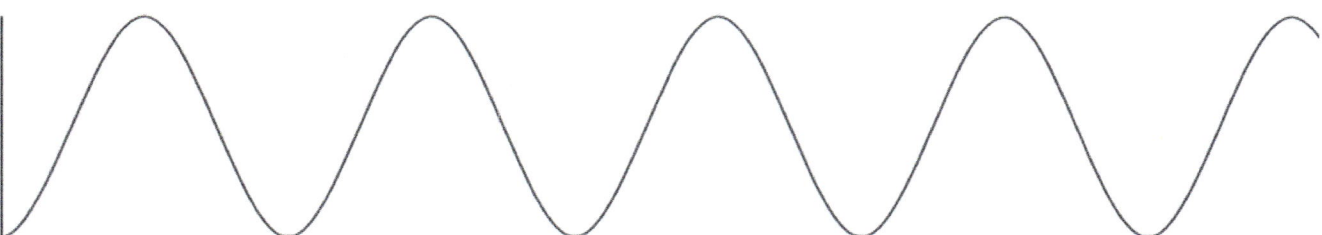

The Second Soundwave.

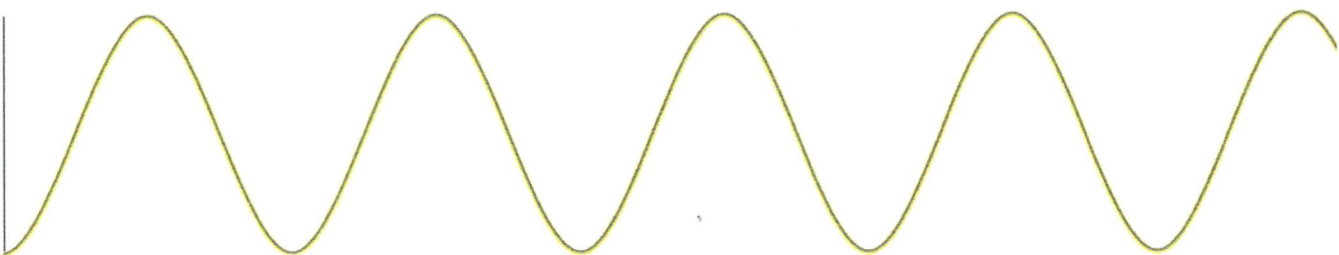

This is the Intial and the Second Soundwave merged together. As you can see, the two soundwaves merge together perfectly.

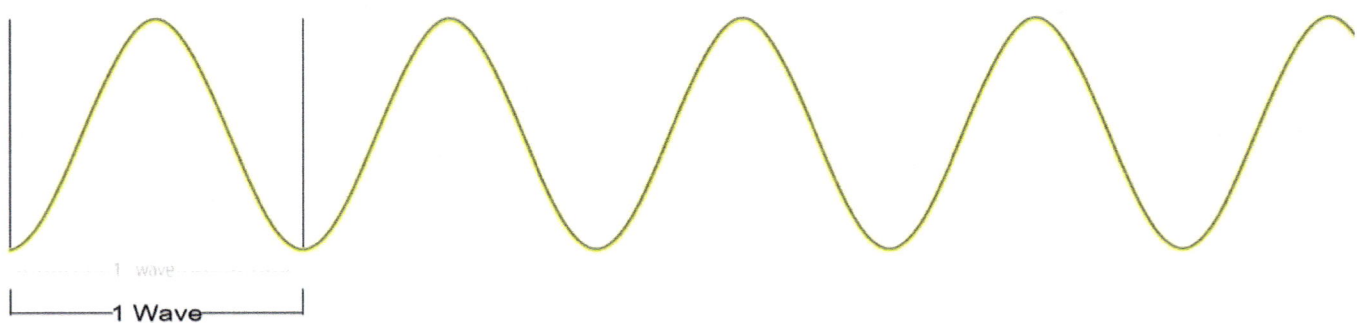

Note: *In mathematical terms we would describe the 'mixture' as a ratio of 1:1 (you read 1:1 as 1 to 1). For every 1 wave of the Initial frequency (the yellow wave) there will be exactly 1 wave of the second frequency (the grey wave).*

If you are not familiar with ratios, a ratio is a mathematical term used to describe how much of one thing there is in comparison to another thing. Don't worry, you won't be expected to calculate ratios; it's just important that you understand what they are.

Examples-

261:261 = 1:1 ratio

185:185 = 1:1 ratio

Note: As the ratio of the mixture decreases (e.g., 1: 0.75 is less than 1: 1), the soundwaves will merge less. The less the soundwaves merge, the more dissonant the mixture will sound. This will be made clearer in our next example.

The second 'mixture' was heard as a Little Less Consonant-

Let's see why:

The frequency of the Initial sound (the Tonal Center) was 261 as marked below by the yellow dot.

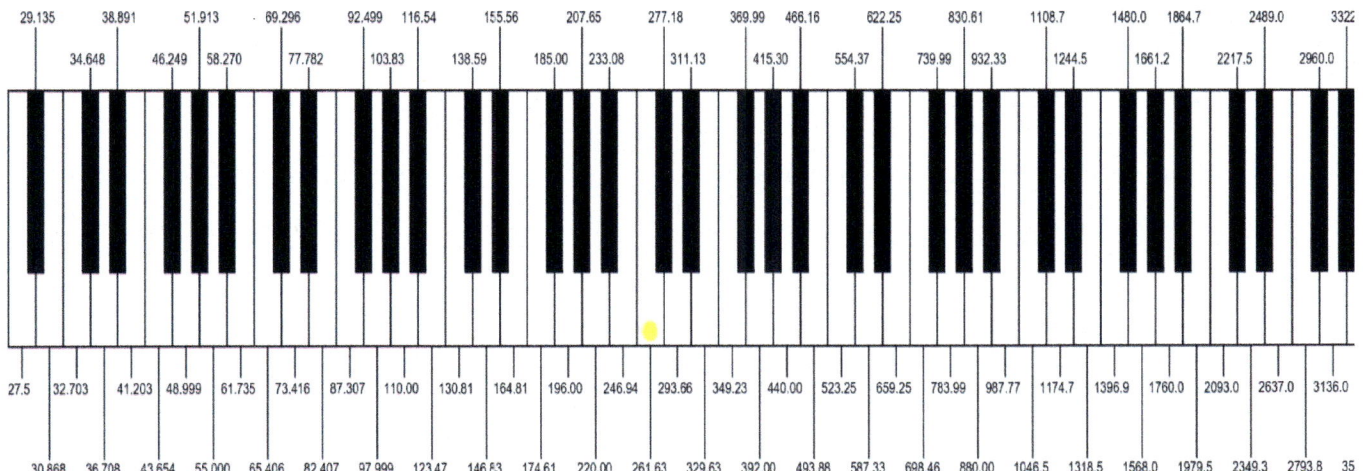

The frequency of the second sound was 196. Marked by the grey dot in the image below.

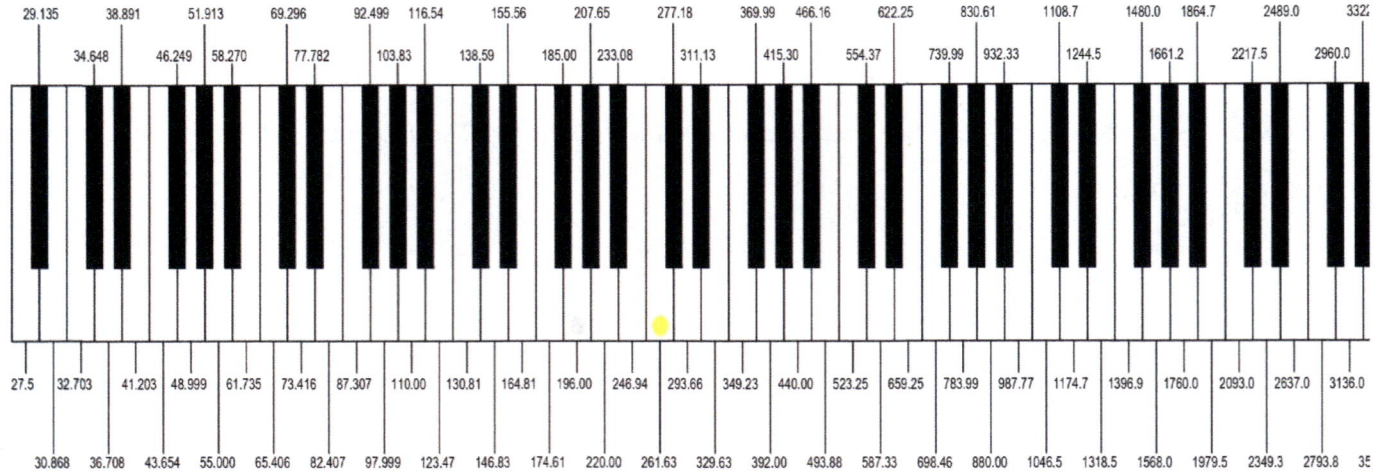

Please, using the index finger from your right hand, **play** the yellow dot, and then using the index finger from your left hand, **play** the grey dot. To hear the sound mixture clearly, I suggest playing the notes separately and then together at least 2 times.

The mixture of these two frequencies was heard as a little less consonant than the first example because these two frequencies merge less often.

Visual depiction-

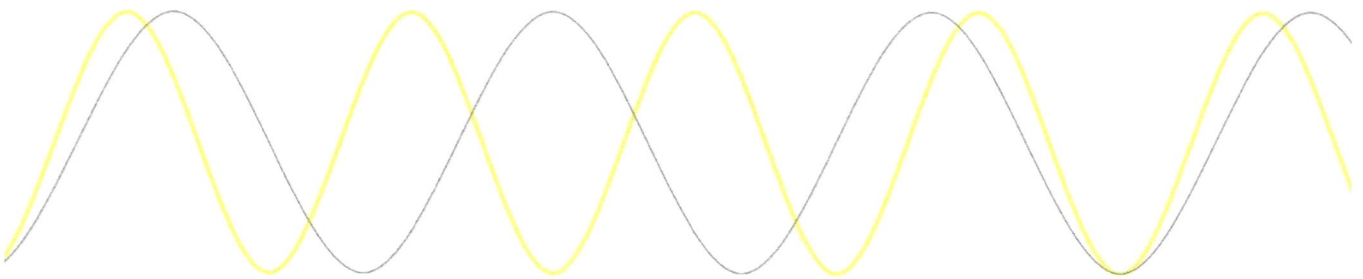

We clearly see that the waves of these two frequencies merge less often than our first example.

Note: *In mathematical terms, we would describe the mixture as a ratio of (261 to 196) or 1: 0.75.*

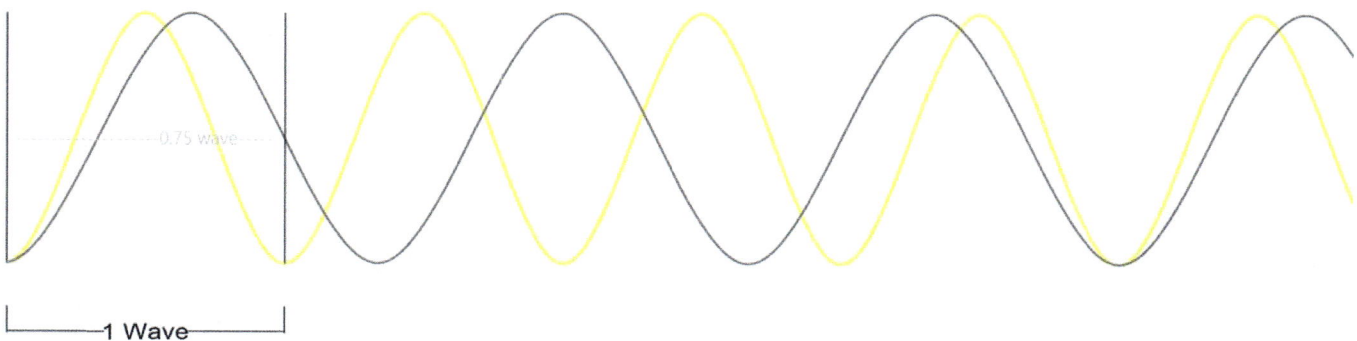

For every 1 wave of the Initial frequency (the yellow wave), there will be 0.75 wave of the second frequency (the grey wave).

Note: *The ratio decreased from 1: 1 to 1: 0.75 causing the soundwaves to merge less and thereby <u>increasing the dissonance</u>*

The third 'mixture' was heard as dissonant.

Let's see why:

The frequency of the Initial sound (the Tonal Center) was 261 as shown by the yellow dot below.

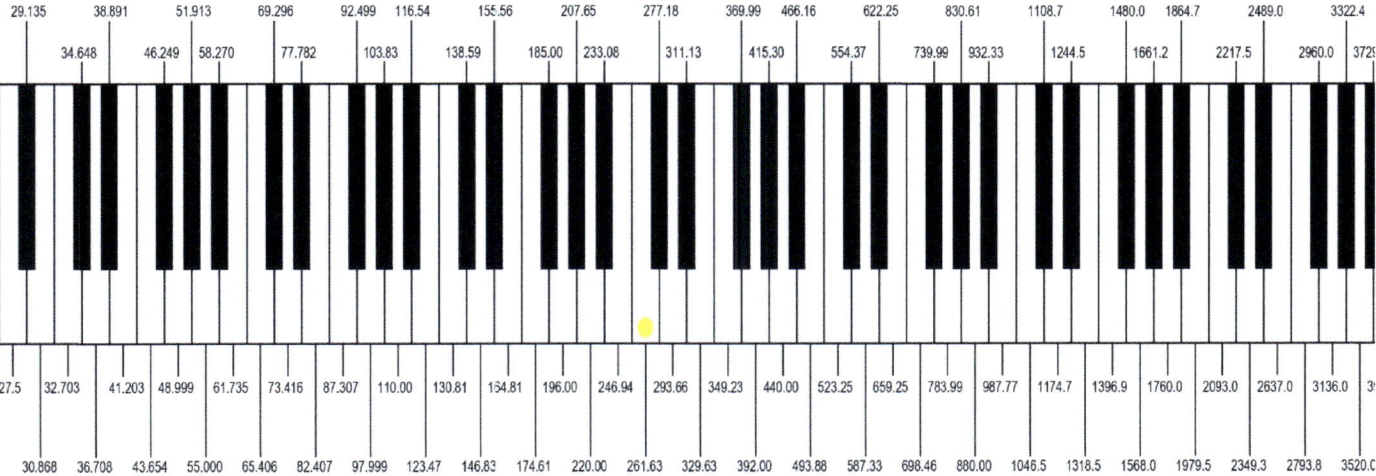

The frequency of the second sound was 92.4. Marked by the grey dot in the image below.

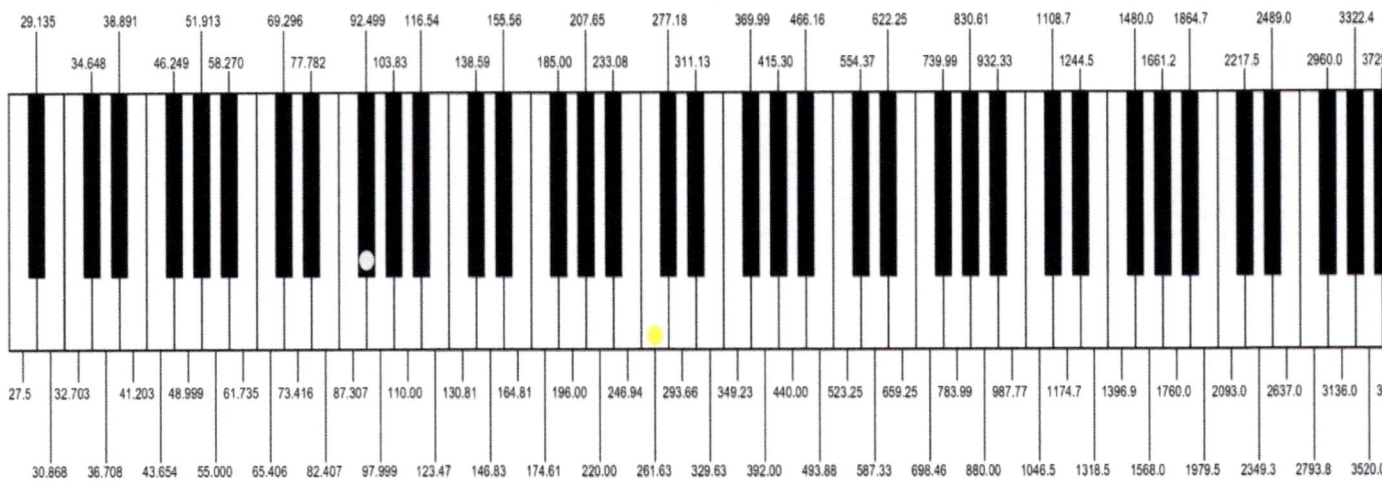

Please, using the index finger from your right hand, **play** the yellow dot, and then using the index finger from your left hand, **play** the grey dot. Again, to hear the sound mixture clearly, I suggest playing the notes separately and then together at least 3 times.

The mixture of these two frequencies was heard as dissonant because the two frequencies barely merge at all.

Visual depiction-

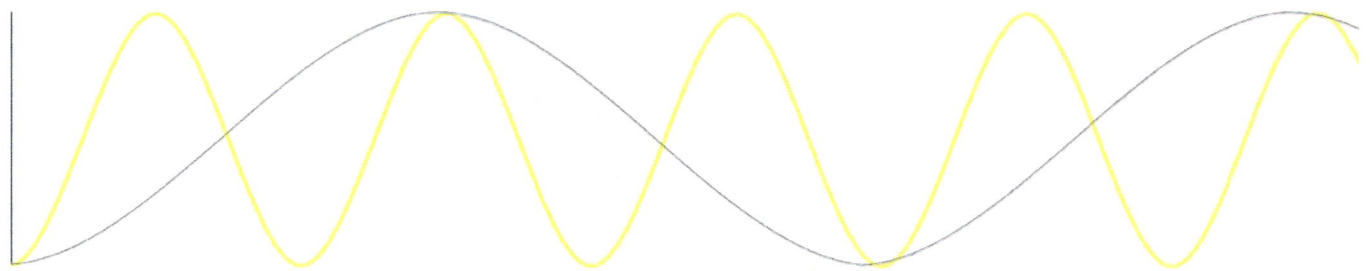

We see clearly that the waves of these two frequencies barely merge at all.

Note: In mathematical terms, we would describe the mixture as a ratio of (261 to 92.4) or 1: 0.34

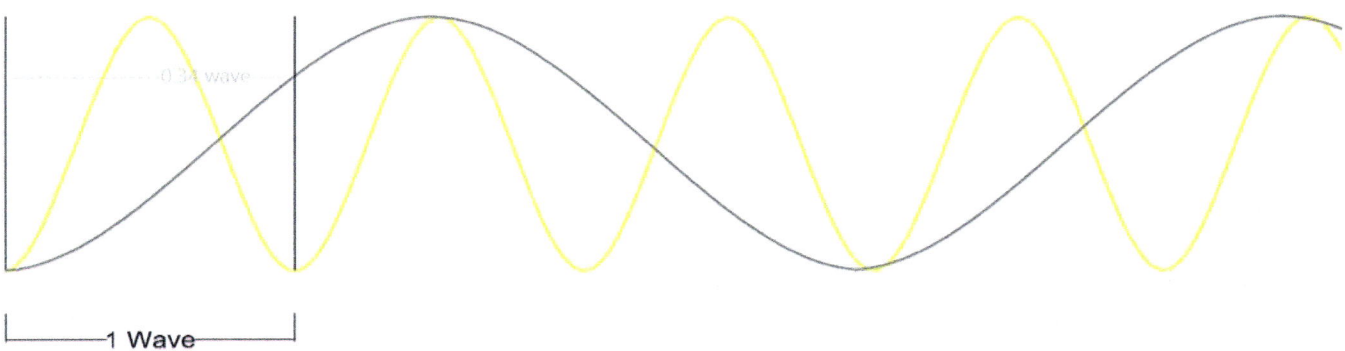

For every 1 wave of the Initial frequency, there will only be 0.34 wave of the second frequency.

Good news! You don't need to memorize any of the ratios. You just need to understand the main concept that <u>when any two notes interact there are two frequencies 'mixing' or 'merging' together.</u>

- *The more the two frequencies merge*, the *more consonant* the mixture will sound
- *The less the two frequencies merge,* the *more dissonant* the mixture will sound

Note: There are 12 notes in our music alphabet, but there are 13 'mixes'. This is because the first mixture is the Initial sound, that by repeating the note, mixes with itself (as we heard in our first sound sample). In the next section I will provide you with all 13 mixes in order, or on a sliding scale, from consonant to dissonant. Then we will learn how many amazing things we can do with the mixtures (i.e., create scales, melodies and harmony sections).

Bonus:

Earlier we learned that when any frequency is doubled or divided, we hear it as different yet similar. This implies that we can double or divide not only the Initial sound of any interacting notes, but also the second sound. For this example, let's use the frequencies 261 and 196. As you will see, this will provide you with multiple ways to play the same mixture.

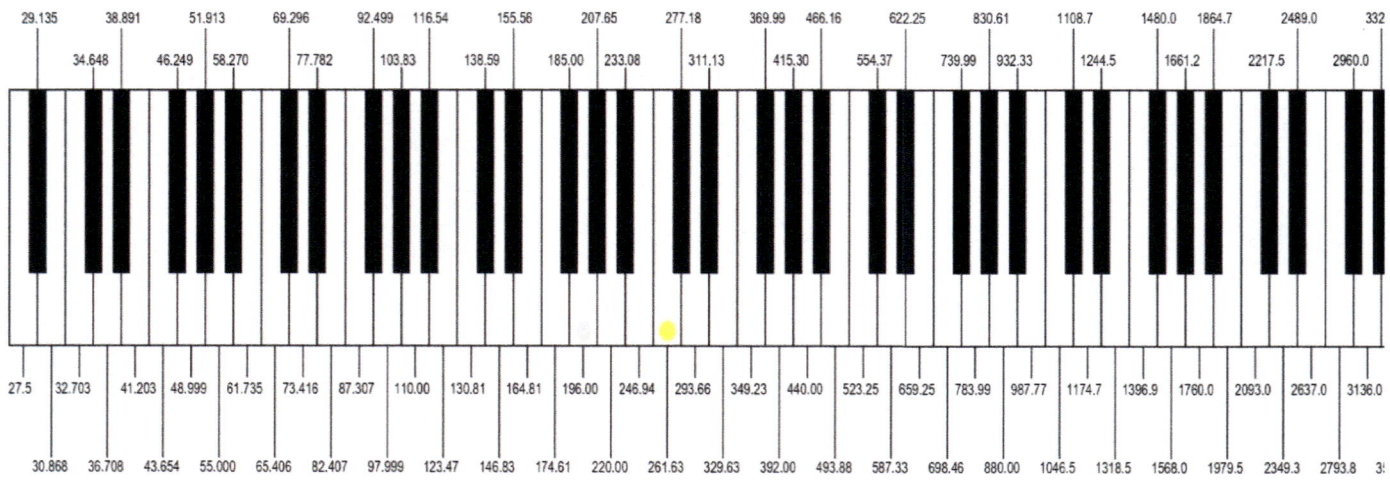

Please, using the index finger from your right hand, **play** the frequency 261. Marked above by the yellow dot. Then using the index finger from your left hand, **play** the frequency 196. Marked by the grey dot. Again, for a better attuned hearing of these sounds, please play the notes together and separately at least 3 times.

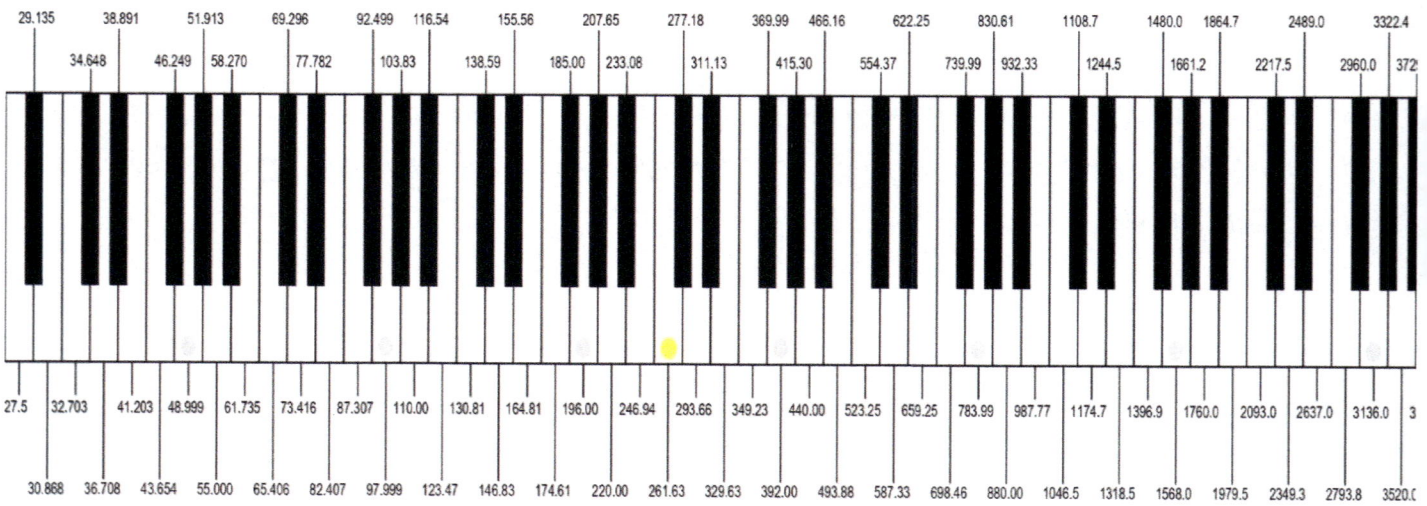

Now, play the yellow dot (261) and starting on 48.9 play each grey dot and ending with 3136. Play each combination separately and then together.

Do you hear both the difference and similarity? It's amazing, right?

Now, please play the sequence again but instead of the grey dot on 392, play the frequency 440.

Do you agree that 440 sounded foreign?

Correct!

When you played the frequency 440, it did not sound similar because the grey dot is not related.

You now have many options to create the same mixture!

Great work!

Please, *review this section before you continue and make sure everything is clear.*

SECTION 4-

In this section I will provide you with all 13 mixes in order from consonant to dissonant. Each mixture has a name that I will introduce you to, as well as the common abbreviations used by musicians.

In all of these examples, the Tonal Center is the same and represented by the yellow dot, the second sound by the grey dot. All the examples will be in the same octave, but as you just learned you can play any of these notes in any octave.

As you go through this list-

- **Use** your index finger from your left hand for the yellow dot, and use your index finger from your right hand for the grey dot.
- **Play** the notes of each mixture separately and together at least three times.
- **Listen** as each mixture progressively 'slides' away from consonance towards dissonance.

Note: You might not fully agree with this list. Similar to vision, in that we all see colors slightly differently, we will all hear sound mixtures slightly differently. If you can, I suggest printing these diagrams out for easy access and for study flashcards. Images and diagrams are free to download from our website-
www.beforeyoulearn.com

1. The first mixture is the most consonant mixture and it is called **Unison**

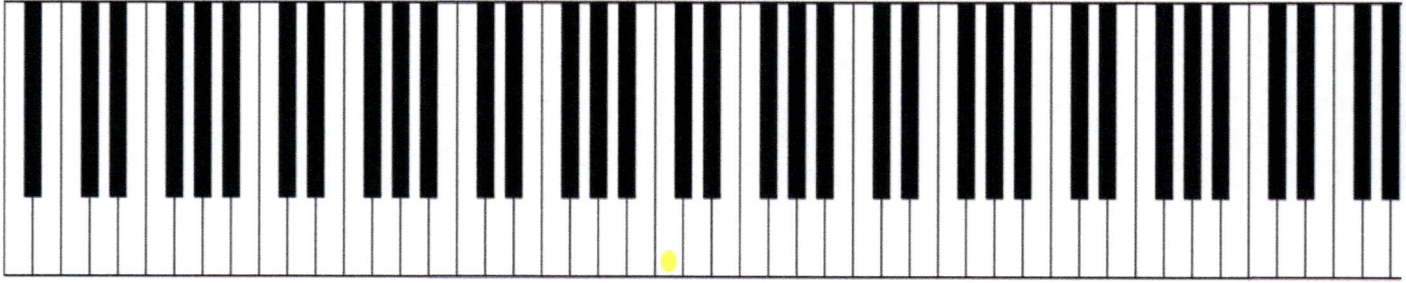

Please play- *for this mixture, simply play and repeat the note of the yellow dot.*

2. This mixture is called an **Octave**

Please play-

3. This mixture is called a **Perfect 5**th

Please play-

4. This mixture is called a **Major 3**rd

Please play-

5. This mixture is called a **Perfect 4ᵗʰ**

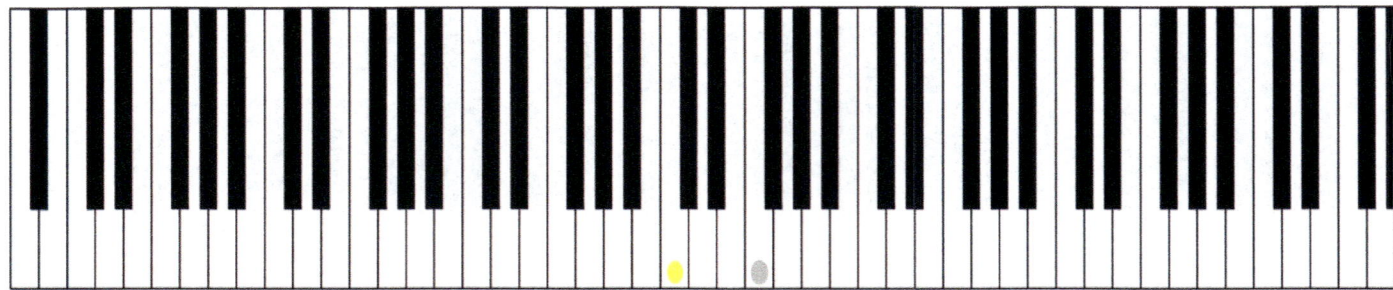

Please play-

6. This mixture is called a **Major 6th**

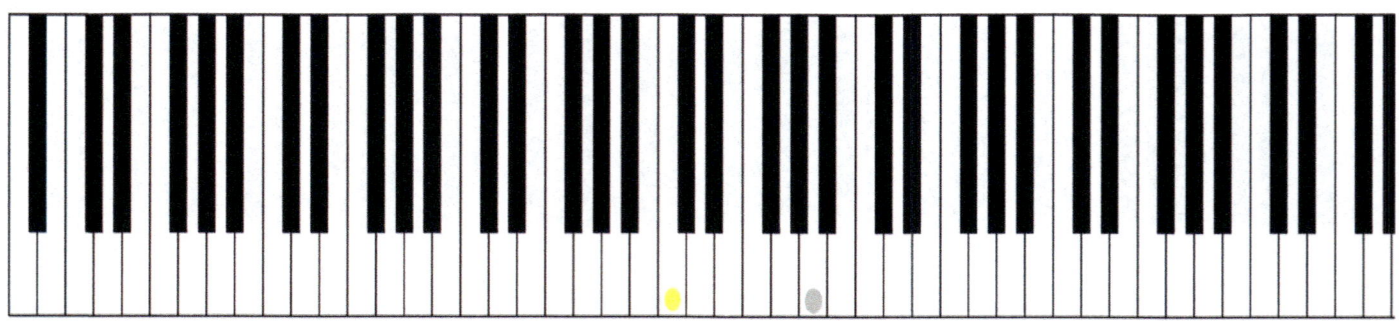

Please play-

7. This mixture is called a **Major 2ⁿᵈ**

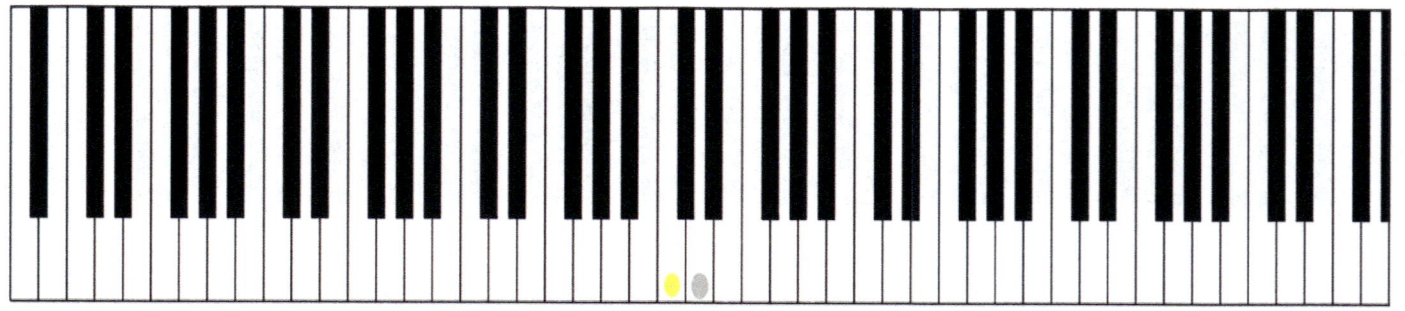

Please play-

8. This mixture is called a **Major 7**th

Please play-

9. This mixture is called a **minor 6**th

Please play-

10. This mixture is called a **minor 3**rd

Please play-

11. This mixture is called a **minor 7th**

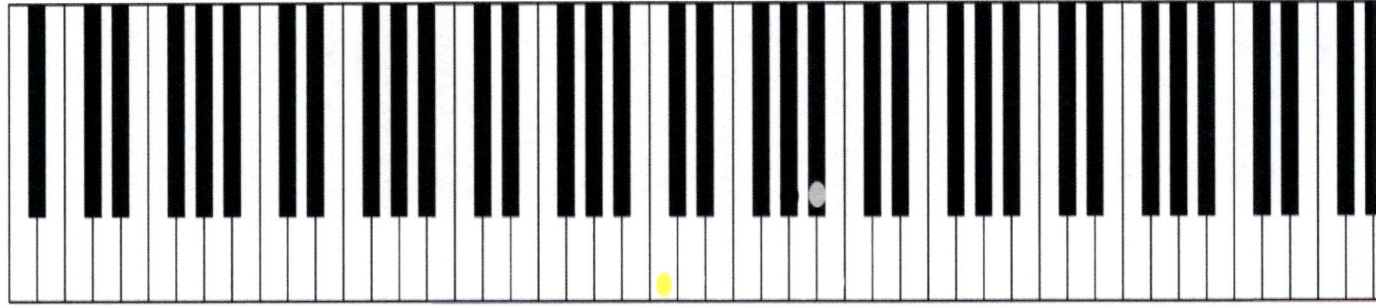

Please play-

12. This mixture is called a **minor 2nd**

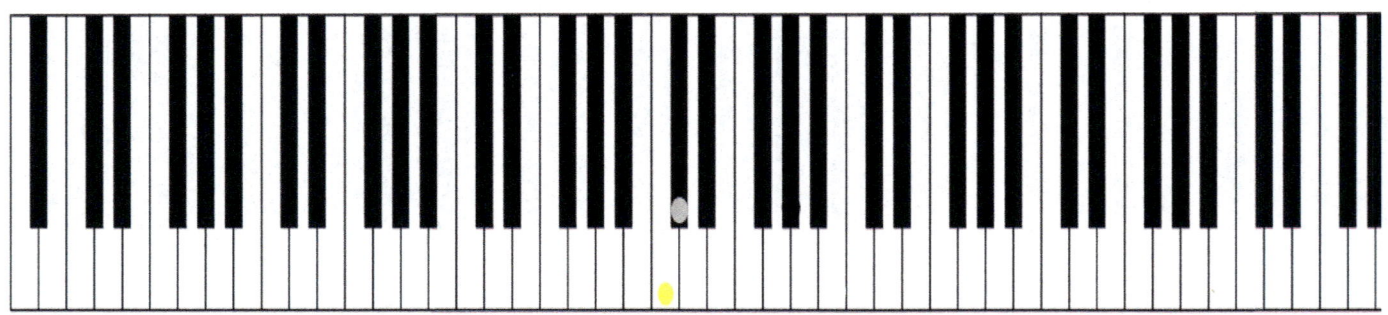

Please play-

13. This mixture is called a **tri-tone:** *This is the most dissonant mixture*

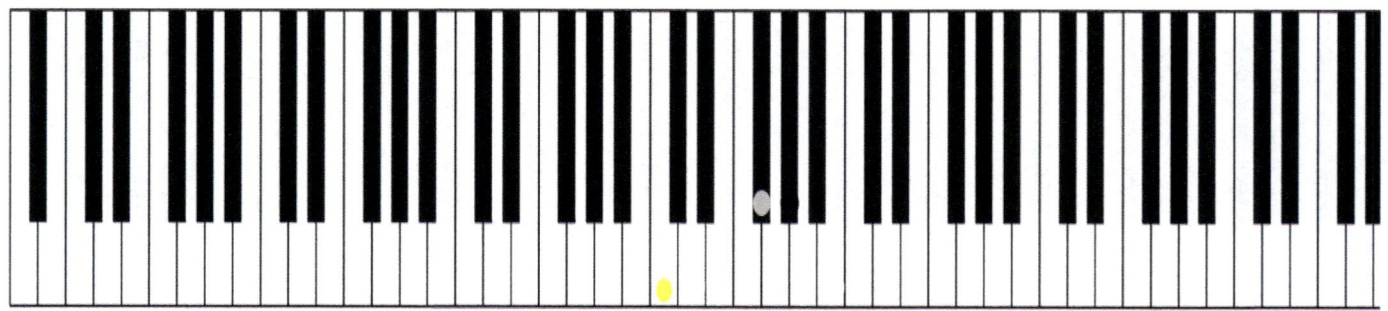

Please play-

Again, due to the fact that we all hear sound slightly different you might have disagreed with certain parts of this list. In order to unmistakably hear the sliding scale of consonance and dissonance, please go back to the top of the list and **play** the mixtures in this order- Octave, Major 3rd, minor 3rd, minor 2nd, tri-tone. I also suggest playing the Octave followed by the tri-tone to hear the contrast between the most consonant and the most dissonant. *By leaving some mixtures out it might be easier for you to hear the contrast in the mixtures.*

Questions:

- As you played, did you hear the mixtures slide from consonance towards dissonance?
- Do you fully understand why each mixture evoked a different feeling, mood, or emotion?
- Is it clear that the mixtures that sounded dissonant had soundwaves that merged less and the mixtures that sounded consonant had soundwaves that merged more?

Great work!

Here are all the mixtures, on a sliding scale, from the most Consonant to the most Dissonant:

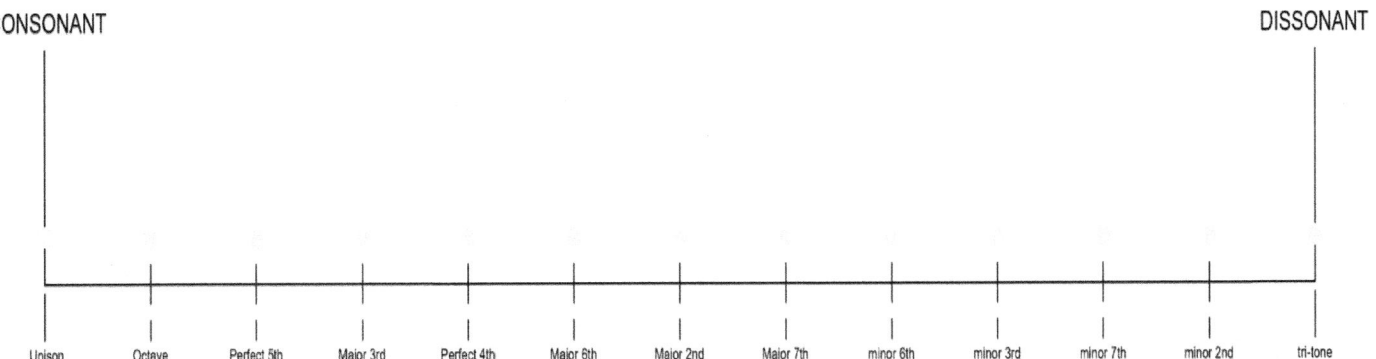

Note: *Generally speaking, Unison through Major 2nd are consonant. Major 7th through tri-tone are dissonant. (For simplicity sake, most musicians group all the Majors together as the consonant intervals and the minors and tri-tone as the dissonat intervals.)*

Let's test our knowledge-

Most of us have heard the theme song to the movie *Jaws*. If you have not heard it, or heard of the movie, Jaws is about a shark that terrorizes a small beach community. The theme song was composed to evoke a sense of terror.

When the theme song starts, we hear two notes, and their mixture, repeating over and over again. Do you think the composer used a consonant or dissonant mixture to evoke the sense of terror?

Correct!

The composer chose a dissonant mixture to evoke a sense of terror. In fact, it is the minor 2nd that is repeated. There are other musical elements that the composer used that added to the sense of terror but for now we are only concerned with the mixture.

Most of us have heard a fire truck blaring its siren as it races towards a fire. The sound of the siren was expressly composed to evoke a sense of emergency. When we hear the siren, we are hearing a mixture of two notes repeating over and over. Do you think the composer used a consonant or a dissonant mixture to evoke a sense of emergency?

Correct!

The composer chose a dissonant mixture to evoke the sense of emergency. In fact most emergency service vehicles use the tri-tone given its piercing dissonance.

Bonus: Now that you know all the mixtures in order from consonant to dissonant, you want to be able to build any mixture starting on any of the 12 notes of the music alphabet (in any octave). How you build any mixture, on any Initial sound, is surprisingly easier than you might think. All we need to do is count the number of piano keys it is from the Initial frequency, **up** to the second sound of any mixture. Then, when you pick a new Initial sound, you simply count **up** the same number of piano keys.

Let me illustrate-

For this example, I will use the mixture of a minor 2nd (but as you will see, this practice works for every one of the 13 mixtures).

minor 2nd-

If we count from the Initial sound (the yellow dot) **up** to the second sound (the grey dot), we see that we have moved up 1 note or, in music terms we say we moved up 1 half-step or 1 semi-tone. These terms are synonyms, for this course we will use the term half-step. So, to create a minor 2nd, on any note in the music alphabet, we only need to move **up** 1 note or 1 half-step.

And…

If we count from the Initial sound (the yellow dot), **down** to the second sound (the grey dot), we see that we moved **down** 11 notes or **down** 11 half-steps.

So, to create a minor 2nd, starting on any note in the music alphabet, we only need to move **up** 1 note or half-step, or **down** 11 notes or 11 half-steps. Rather than counting down 11 notes, it might be quicker to identify a landmark.

Try it out:

Pick any note on the piano as your new Initial sound, then go **up** 1 half-step or go **down** 11 half-steps.

Example-

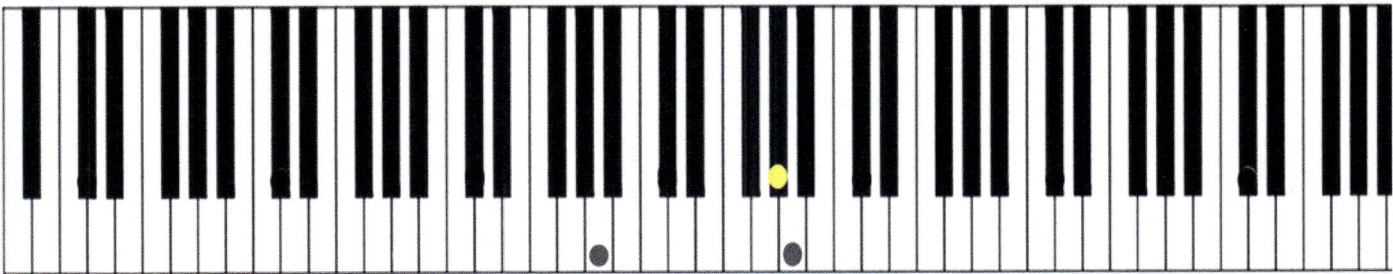

I picked a 'new Initial' and moved **up** 1 half-step and moved **down** 11 half-steps.

Please, build and play a minor 2nd on at least 2 different Initial sounds. Don't forget that instead of counting down 11 half-steps you could use a landmark. As you play, experiment playing the notes in the mixture separately and then together, in multiple octaves. Take your time, relax, and try to close your eyes to really hear the sound, feeling, and mood of this mixture. Furthermore, find the octave that you like best- *there is no right or wrong answer.*

The chart below will tell you how to create any mixture starting from any note on the piano. We will use this chart to create some mixtures later, for now just take a look. *Again, I suggest printing the diagrams and charts out for easy access and for study flashcards. Images and diagrams are free to download from our website-* www.beforeyoulearn.com

To create the mixture,	move this number of steps	Common abbreviations
Unison	0 Half Steps	U
Octave	12 Half Steps up- or 12 down	8va
Perfect 5th	7 Half Step up- or 5 down	P5
Major 3rd	4 Half Steps up- or 8 down	MJ3
Perfect 4th	5 Half Steps up- or 7 down	P4
Major 6th	9 Half Steps up- or 3 down	MJ6
Major 2nd	2 Half Steps up- or 10 down	MJ2
Major 7th	11 Half Steps up- or 1 down	MJ7
minor 6th	8 Half Steps up- or 4 down	mi6
minor 3rd	3 Half Steps up- or 9 down	mi3
minor 7th	10 Half Steps up- or 2 down	mi7
minor 2nd	1 half step up- or 11 down	mi2
tri-tone	6 Half Steps up- or 6 down	tt

This will be one of your greatest tools but with consistent practice at the keyboard all of this will become second nature to you and you will no longer need to refer to this table.

Note: Since every mixture has two notes that are some distance or some **Interval** apart, musicians refer to these mixtures as **Intervals**. For the rest of this pre-requisite course, we too will be referring to mixtures as **Intervals**. (If you can, I suggest printing the above chart for easy access and for a study guide.)

So, the only difference we need to make is to replace the term Mixture, with the more formal term **Interval**

To create the Interval	move this number of steps...	common abbreviations
Unison	0 Half Steps	U
Octave	12 Half Steps up- or 12 down	8va
Perfect 5th	7 Half Step up- or 5 down	P5
Major 3rd	4 Half Steps up- or 8 down	MJ3
Perfect 4th	5 Half Steps up- or 7 down	P4
Major 6th	9 Half Steps up- or 3 down	MJ6
Major 2nd	2 Half Steps up- or 10 down	MJ2
Major 7th	11 Half Steps up- or 1 down	MJ7
minor 6th	8 Half Steps up- or 4 down	mi6
minor 3rd	3 Half Steps up- or 9 down	mi3
minor 7th	10 Half Steps up- or 2 down	mi7
minor 2nd	1 half step up- or 11 down	mi 2
tri-tone	6 Half Steps up- or 6 down	tt

Let's have some fun!

As you play, try to keep your body relaxed and your breath calm. You are experimenting so there is no pressure to create a perfect sound. You're asked to play 2 examples but of course your encouraged to try more!

Pick any consonant interval from the chart (e.g., one between Unison and Major 2nd). Write down how many half steps, either up or down, are needed to create the interval. Then, **pick** any note on the piano as your Initial tone and apply the number of steps needed, either up or down, to **play** the interval.

Please, play the interval that you chose. Play the interval in multiple octaves up and down the piano. Create a landmark to help guide you.

Feel free to play the notes of the interval separately and together. Again, just allow yourself to experiment.

Now, for contrast, **please pick** any dissonant interval from the chart above (i.e., between Major 7 and tri-tone). Write down how many half-steps, either up or down are needed to create the interval. Then, **pick** any note on the piano as your Initial tone and apply the number of steps needed, either up or down, to create the interval.

Please, play the interval that you chose. Play the interval in multiple octaves up and down the piano. Create a landmark to help guide you.

Note: Not only do you know why the interval that you chose evokes its feeling, mood, or emotion- you can create it starting on any note on the piano; either by counting half-steps, or using landmarks!

Very Impressive Work!

Intervals are a Music Element:

Like every other music element, we have discussed so far, Intervals provide us with a range for us to interplay with. In my opinion, intervals are the most important music element. As you will see, intervals are applicable to every music element that has multiple notes interacting (i.e., scales, melody, harmony sections).

This is where the fun really begins!

Let's add our new music elements (i.e., octaves and intervals) to the musical blueprint and construct two very simple compositions and compare- *Remember, you do not need to play these two compositions; it is equally valuable to imagine how these compositions would sound.*

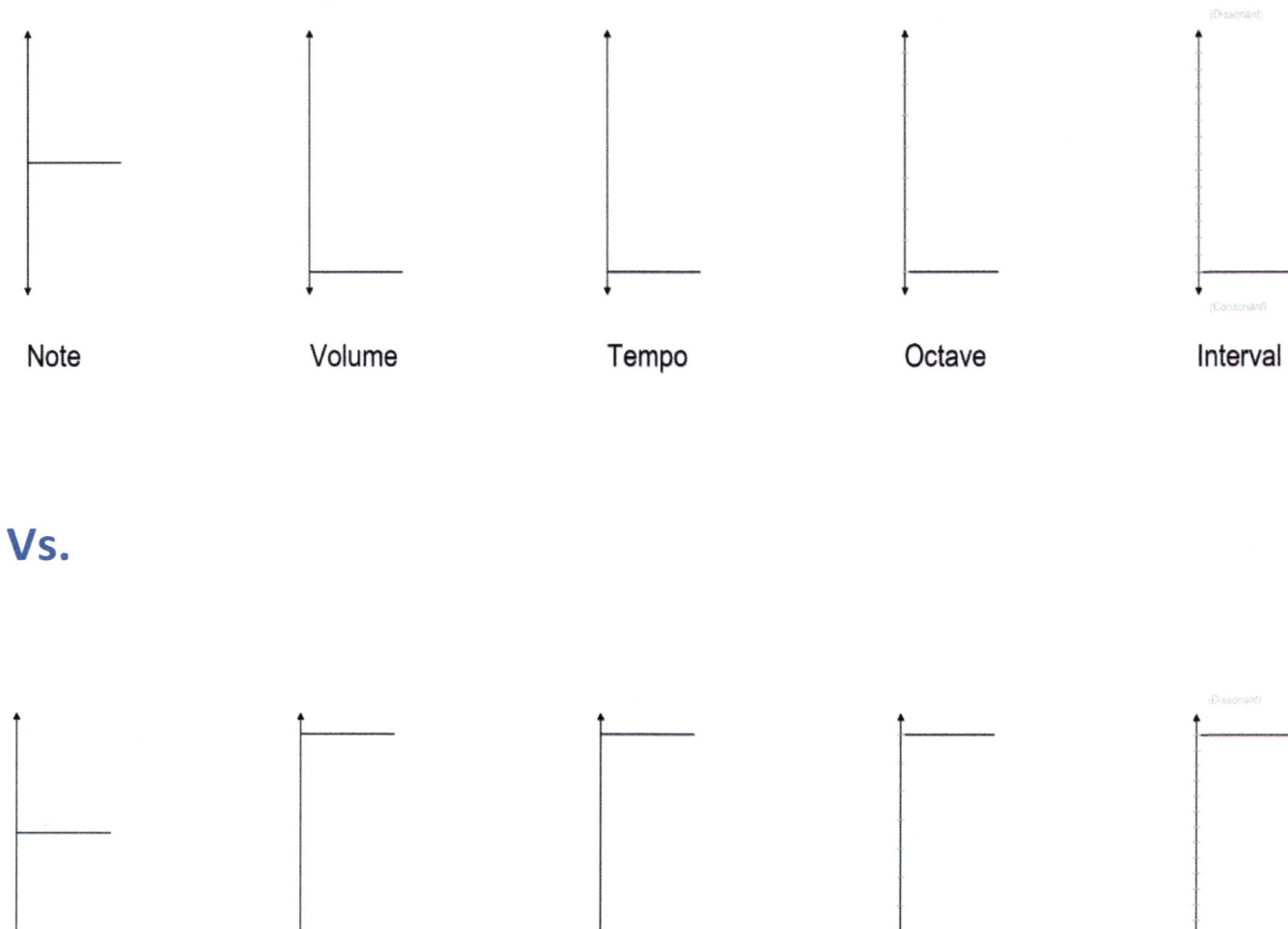

Vs.

We see that both compositions are going to use the same Initial note.

- The first composition has a very low volume, a very slow tempo, uses the notes from the first octave (notes with a slow vibration or low frequency), and uses a consonant interval

- The second composition has a very high volume, an extremely fast tempo, uses the notes from the last octave (notes with a fast vibration or high frequency), and uses a dissonant interval

It should be clear that we would get two completely different outcomes. They are different for one reason and one reason alone: *Music is the interplay of consonance and dissonance.*

Each composition shows a different 'interplay' of music elements; therefore, each composition evokes a different feeling, mood, or emotion.

Despite adding more music elements, the **questions** we asked earlier are still relevant.

- Which composition would you choose to fall asleep or relax to?
- Which composition would you choose to get energized?

Do you see that both compositions could be perceived as either consonant or dissonant depending on the Context?

-If you were trying to relax, the first composition would be perceived as consonant.

-If you wanted to be energized, the first composition would be perceived as dissonant.

And vice versa.

Note: *As we continue to add more elements (or more information) to the blueprint, it will become increasingly cluttered and difficult to read. Luckily, there is a more efficient way for us to notate our music making. It's called Sheet Music. We will learn how to transfer the information from a musical blueprint to sheet music in another course.*

Excellent Work!

Please, *review this section before you continue and make sure everything is clear.*

SECTION 5-

Let's apply the Principles of Sound and Intervals to create Scales-

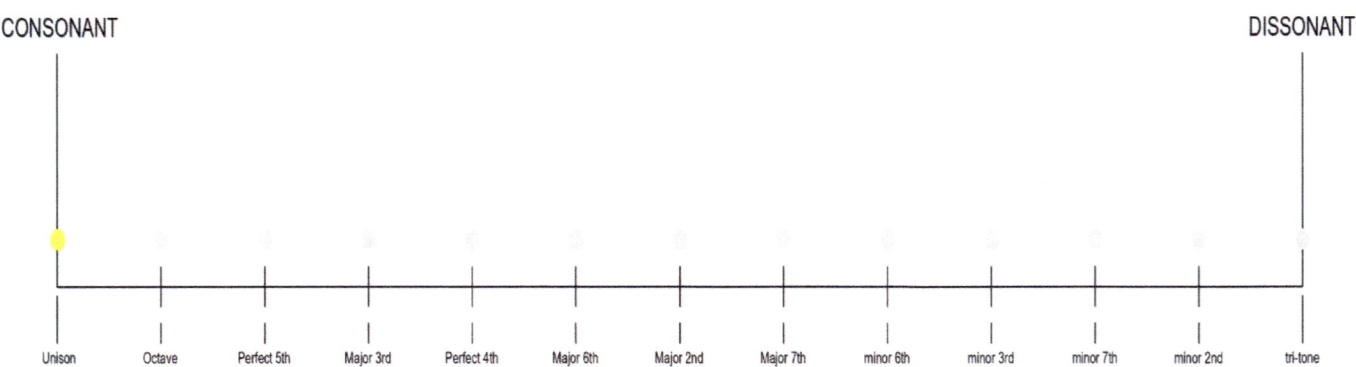

There are 13 Intervals in our music alphabet (image above); each having the ability to evoke its own feeling, mood, or emotion. Instead of always using all 13 intervals, in a composition, the composer can choose what intervals they want to use; in order to evoke the desired feeling, mood, or emotion. *Similar to a chef choosing ingredients for a recipe.*

We call these subsets **Scales.**

Just as each interval can evoke its own feeling, mood, or emotion, so too can each scale.

Note: *Scales can have any number of intervals in them. As you will see in upcoming examples, some scales have 4 intervals and some have 6 intervals etc. The most commonly known and used scales have 7 intervals. You might have heard of the Major or minor Scale. We will explore them a little later.*

Furthermore, The Ancient Greeks believed deeply in the ability of certain scales to communicate different feelings, moods, and emotions. In fact, they assigned different scales for different occasions. We will explore this further in the Music History section.

Let's create and compare the overall feeling, mood and emotion of 3 different Scales-

Note: There are more than 3 scales in existence; we are just starting with three. Rest assured that what you are about to learn is applicable to every scale that has ever been created or ever will be created. The first scale will be comprised of 5 intervals. The second will have 4 intervals and the last will have 6 intervals.

The First Scale: (The name is not important at this time.)

This scale consists of 5 consonant intervals- Unison, Perfect 5th, Major 3rd, Major 6th, and Major 2nd

Remember, when you repeat the Tonal Center, you are playing a Unison interval.

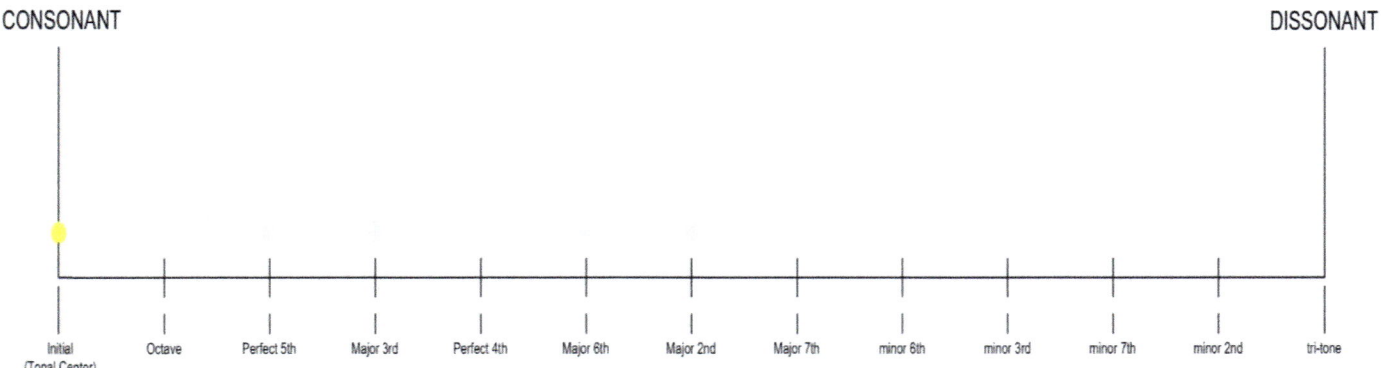

As you can see, in the diagram above, the intervals in this scale are consonant. *Remember that as a general rule, Unison through Major 2nd are consonant.* So, we should already be able to make some predictions as to how this scale will sound.

Note: Earlier, we said that the brain does not need to hear the two frequencies of an interval simultaneously in order to recognize it. In fact, and admittingly this is hard to comprehend, as soon as the Tonal Center is played-our brain will mix every new note in the scale with it even if the tonal center is not repeated. It's as if the brain, whether the Tonal Center is being played or not, hears it continuously playing. Little is known as to how the brain does this. This will become clear in a moment

Please, using only your index finger from your right hand, **play** these notes in order. Play one note at a time, from left to right, starting on the yellow dot (261).

As you play, try to keep your body relaxed and your breath calm. Play as many times as needed so that finding the notes becomes easy. The less energy you use to find the notes, the more energy you will have to connect to the sound and the overall vibe of the scale.

I suggest playing the scale at least 3 times. You might want to play the scale forwards and backwards 2 times, then on your 3rd time try and continue playing the scale up into all the higher octaves.

Make a note of how this scale makes you feel, we are going to compare the sound of this scale to the next two.

Questions:

- Would you agree that this scale sounds consonant?
- Do you fully understand that it sounds consonant because of the consonant intervals in it?

Great!

Now let's compare it to the feeling, mood and emotion of a 4-note Scale-

This Scale consists of 4 intervals: Unison, Major 6th, minor 3rd, and tri-tone.

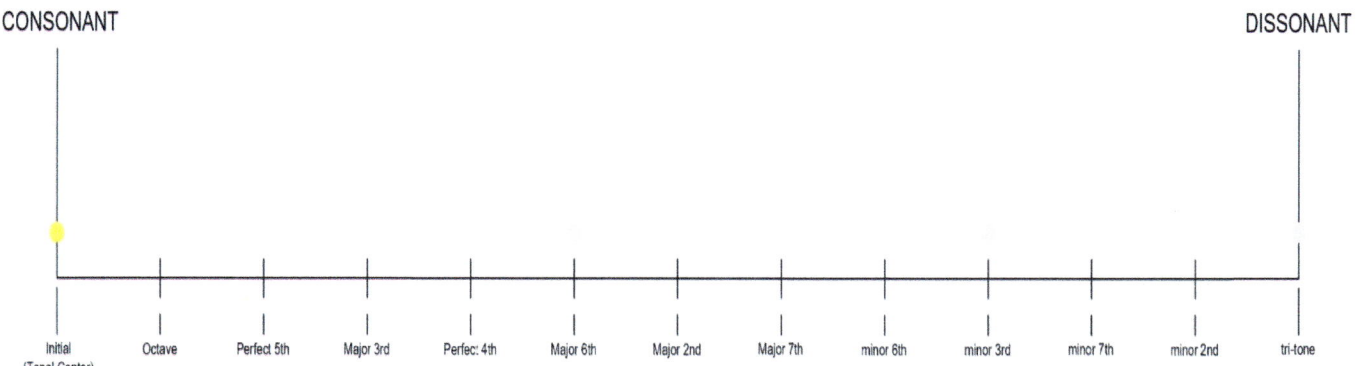

Whereas our first scale consisted entirely of consonant intervals, this scale contains two dissonant intervals. In fact, this scale includes the most dissonant interval, the tri-tone. So, we should already be able to make an educated guess as to how this scale will sound compared to the first scale.

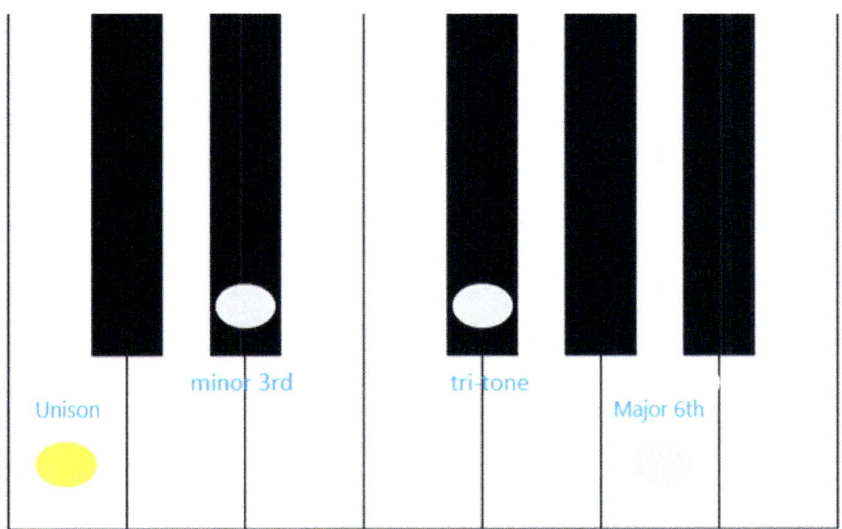

Please, using only your index finger, **play** these notes in order. Play one note at a time, starting on the yellow dot. Again, *as you play, try to keep your body relaxed and your breath calm. Play as many times as needed so that finding the notes becomes easy. The less energy you use to find the notes, the more energy you will have to connect to the sound and the overall vibe of the scale.*

To get the overall feeling, mood, and emotion of this scale, I suggest playing the scale at least 3 times. You might want to play the scale forwards and backwards 2 times, then on your 3rd time try and continue playing the scale up into all the higher octaves.

Questions:

- Would you agree that this scale sounds more dissonant than the first example?
- Do you fully understand that it sounds more dissonant because of the dissonant intervals in it?

Great!

Now let's compare it to a 6-note Scale-

This Scale consists of 6 intervals: Unison, Major 3rd, Major 2nd, minor 6th, minor 7th and the tri-tone.

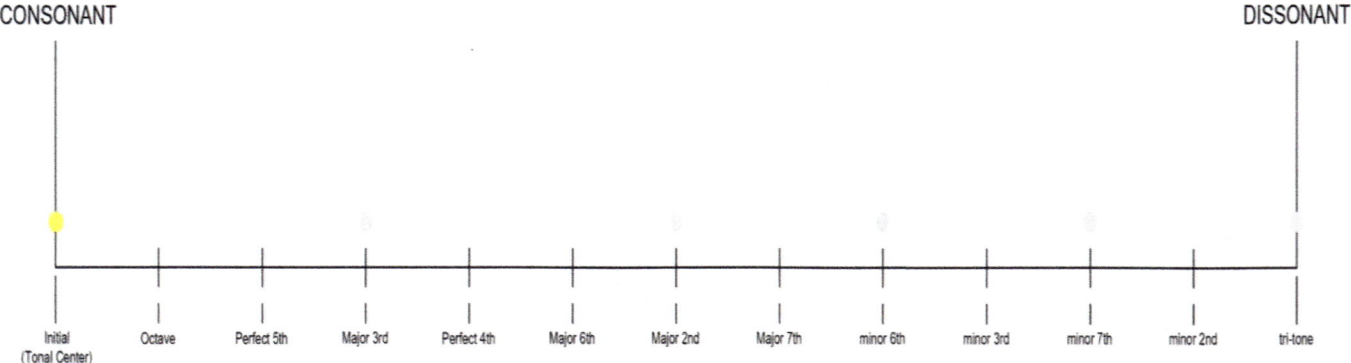

This scale has 6 intervals, 3 of which are consonant and 3 dissonant. Can you make a prediction as to how this scale will sound?

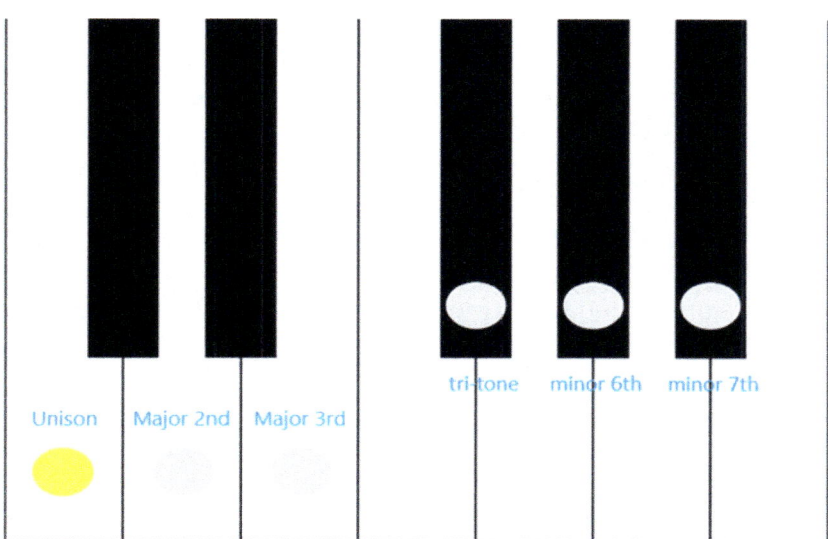

Please, using only your index finger, **play** these notes in order, one note at a time, starting on the yellow dot.

Again, to get the overall feeling, mood, and emotion of this scale, I suggest playing the scale at least 3 times: first play the scale forwards and backwards a couple of times, and then on your 3rd time continue playing the scale up into the higher octaves.

Questions:

How would you describe the overall feeling, mood, or emotion of this scale?

Would you agree that this scale sounds ambiguous? – *This scale doesn't sound particularly consonant or dissonant because it's a perfect blend of consonant and dissonant intervals.*

It should be clear that each scale sounded and evoked a different feeling, mood, or emotion because of the intervals it used. This is true for every scale that has ever been or ever will be created.

When you truly understand that the intervals in a scale give it its distinct sound you will never be intimidated to learn any scale. Now, you can approach any new scale with confidence by simply asking, "What are the Intervals in the Scale?"

Let's test our knowledge-

If you wanted to relax or meditate, would you use the consonant, dissonant or an ambiguous scale? Which of the above scales would you use?

Correct!

You would use the consonant scale to evoke a relaxed, meditative mood. In fact the 5-note scale is called the Major Pentatonic Scale. It happens to be the most widely used scale in the world because of its pleasing sound. Furthermore, if you have ever enjoyed the sounds of windchimes, you were listening to the 5 consonant intervals of the Major Pentatonic Scale!

If you wanted to evoke a sense of terror, like in the theme song for Jaws, would you use a consonant, dissonant or an ambiguous scale? Which of the above scales would you use?

Correct!

You would use the dissonant scale to evoke a sense of terror.

Truly great work!

Bonus: Lets learn two more scales-

Earlier we briefly mentioned that the most commonly used scales consist of 7 intervals. The most popular is the **Major Scale** (also known as the Ionian Scale). It consists of all 7 consonant intervals.

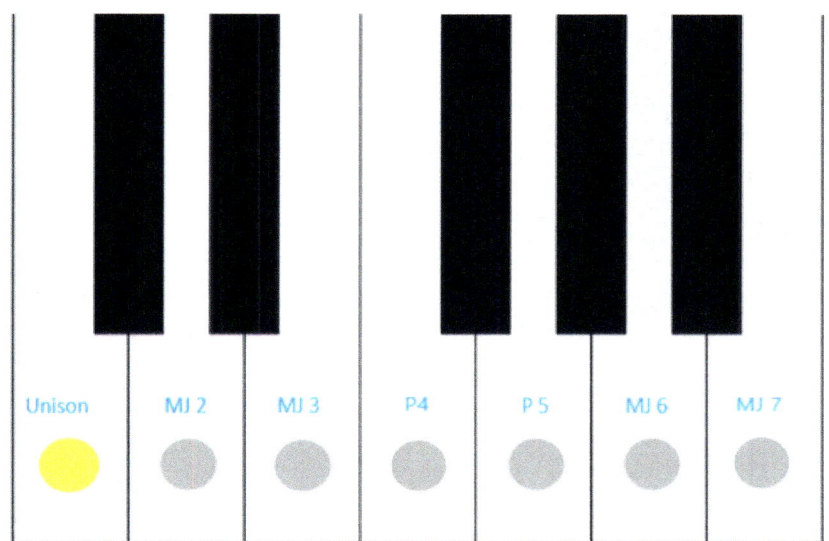

Please, using only your index finger, **play** each note of the scale in order, one note at a time, starting on the yellow dot. *As you play, try to keep your body relaxed and your breath calm. Play as many times as needed so that finding the notes becomes easy. The less energy you use to find the notes, the more energy you will have to connect to the sound and the overall vibe of the scale.*

Again, to get the overall feeling, mood, and emotion of the scale, I suggest playing the scale at least 3 times: first play the scale forwards and backwards a couple of times, and then on your 3rd time continue playing the scale up into the higher octaves.

As an **Added Bonus**, experiment using the pedal that is under your piano or keyboard- *(if you are playing a piano I am talking about the pedal on the right)*. This is called the sustain pedal; when you stepdown on the pedal the note you're playing will continue to sound (ring on) even after you have taken your finger off the piano key. As you will see the pedal adds a wonderful effect. Also, as a reminder, feel free to vary the volume of any of the notes-this is simply done by varying how hard you press down on the piano key. For the remainder of the course, please experiment with the pedal and volume.

The second most popular is the **minor Scale**- (also known as the Aeolian Scale). It consists of 4 consonant intervals and 3 dissonant.

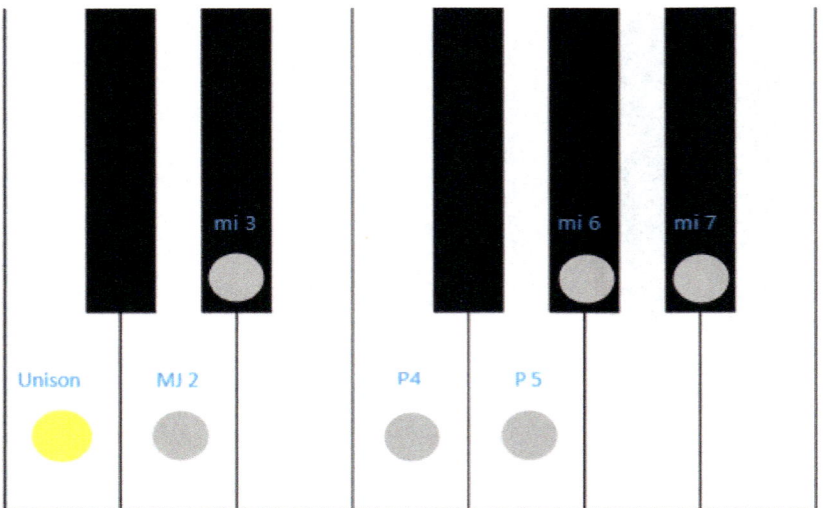

Please, using only your index finger, **play** each note of the scale in order, one note at a time, starting on the yellow dot.

Again, to get the overall feeling, mood, and emotion of the scale, I suggest playing the scale at least 3 times: first play the scale forwards and backwards a couple of times, and then on your 3rd time continue playing the scale up into the higher octaves. Don't forget to experiment with the pedal and volume of your notes.

Questions:

Which of these two scales do you think is used for the song- Happy Birthday?

Correct!

The Major Scale is used.

You're really getting it!

Let's learn how you create any Scale starting on any note-

Now that you know how and why every scale ever created can evoke a range of feelings, moods, and emotions, we want to be able to build any scale starting on any Initial sound- or any of the 12 notes of the music alphabet.

How we build any Scale, on any Initial sound, is surprisingly easier than you might think. It works exactly the same way you created intervals from any given note.

All we need to do is count the number of piano keys it is from the Initial frequency **up** to every interval in the scale. Whichever Initial sound you pick; you simply count up the correct number of piano keys for the designated intervals.

Let me illustrate-

For this example, I will use the 5-note scale (but as you will see, this method works for every scale)

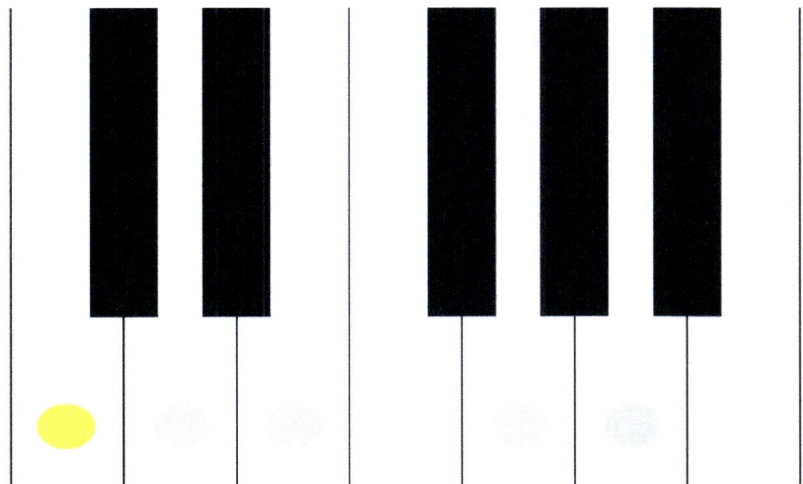

The Initial tone (identified by the yellow dot) to the second note, is 2 half-steps or 1 whole step. In music terms, 2 half-steps are referred to as 1 whole-step.

The second note to the third note, is 2 half-steps-or 1 whole-step. Note: you might encounter the term 'whole-tone' instead of 'whole-step'. They are synonyms; for this course we will use 'whole-step'.

The third to the fourth note, is 3 half-steps or 1 whole and a half-step

And the fourth note to the fifth note, is 2 half-steps or 1-whole-step

In brief, the scale's progression goes like this:

1. Initial note
2. Up 1 whole step
3. Up 1 whole step
4. Up 1 whole and a half-step
5. Up 1 whole-step

*Note: This is the formula needed to create this scale starting on any note of the music alphabet. This formula is aptly named the **Intervallic Formula.***

So, to create the 5-note scale (The Major Pentatonic) starting on any note of the music alphabet, you simply apply the *Intervallic Formula.*

Example-

I picked a new Initial note (the yellow dot) and applied the Intervallic Formula of the Major Pentatonic Scale

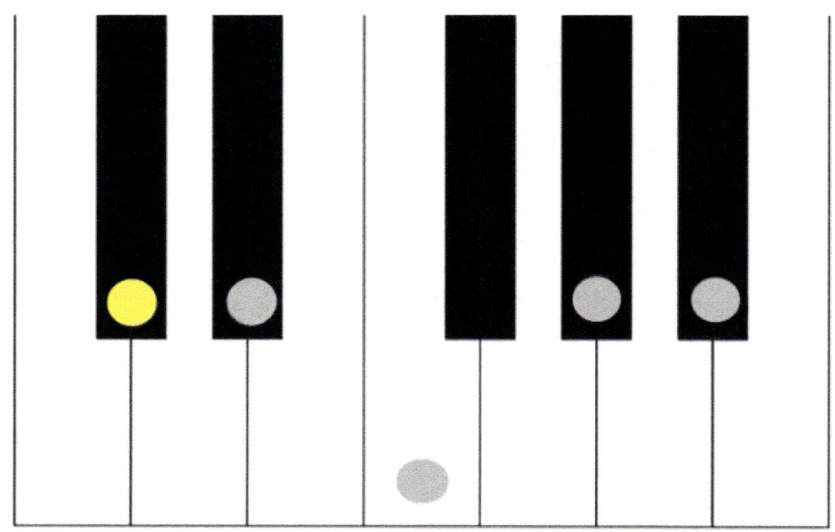

Starting from the 'new' Initial note (the yellow dot) apply the Intervallic Formula-

1. Initial note
2. Up 1 whole step
3. Up 1 whole step
4. Up 1 whole and a half-step
5. Up 1 whole-step.

Please, Play both scales back-to-back.

Do you hear the difference and similarity? Isn't that fascinating?

Note: *Both examples are Major Pentatonic Scales because they both have the same intervals in them (the same Intervallic Formula). The only difference is that we started on a 'new' Initial sound. Feel free to experiment creating the Major Pentatonic, or any of the scales, on any other 'new' Initial Sound.*

Let's recap-

Scales are a Music Element and like every other music element we have discussed so far, scales provide us with a range, or a variety, for us to interplay with.

Excellent work!

Bonus: You might have thought that there aren't many songs that use the notes of a scale in this regimented order, and you would be correct. However, the good news is that even though in most songs the intervals are out of order your brain is still able to recognize the scale. Little is known as to how the brain does this, but it is akin to how we can recognize words out of order. Amnazig ist'n , it? Our brain has seen the words 'amazing, isn't it?' so many times that it will recognize the phrase even if the letters are out of order!

Let's have some fun!

Pick any of the scales from above, and using only your index finger **play** the notes of the scale in order. Remind yourself of the overall feeling, mood, and emotion of this scale and familiarize yourself with the notes. Now, using the same finger from your right hand, **play** the notes of the scale out of order. Just randomly play the notes of the scale in one octave and then, when you are confident, play random notes of the scale in multiple octaves. As you play, try to keep your body relaxed and your breath calm. You are experimenting so there is no pressure to create a perfect sound. Don't forget to experiment with the pedal as well as varying the volume.

Do you agree that even out of order you can still recognize the overall feeling, mood, and emotion of the scale?

What we do know is that as you play the scale out of order the brain is comparing every new sound to the Initial/Tonal Center. Remember, the Tonal Center is the environment or the Context in which we experience every sound that follows. The best way to think of this is that as you are playing randomly, the Tonal Center is being "played" continuously. It's as if the brain, whether the Tonal Center is being played or not hears it continuously playing. Again, little is known as to how the brain does this.

Note: *You might have noticed that as you played freely you liked some of what you played and disliked some of what you played. That is only natural. Please don't underestimate the power of experimenting. Master musicians have used this technique for centuries. It is a way to practice, grow and get well acquainted with the instrument without pressure. When you learn how to read and write music you will be able to catalogue the ideas you like so that you can share and replay them at a later date.*

Great work!

Let's use the musical blueprint and our new music element (i.e., scales) to construct two very simple compositions and compare- *Remember-you do not need to play these two compositions; it is equally valuable to imagine how these compositions would sound. Note: We don't have to list intervals as a separate music element because they are already embedded in the scale.*

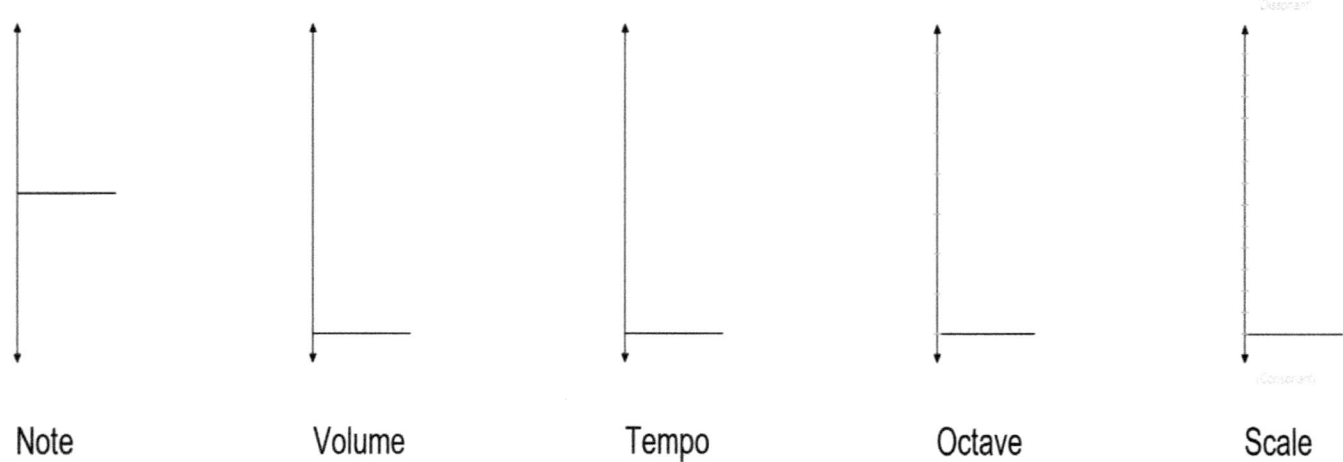

Vs.

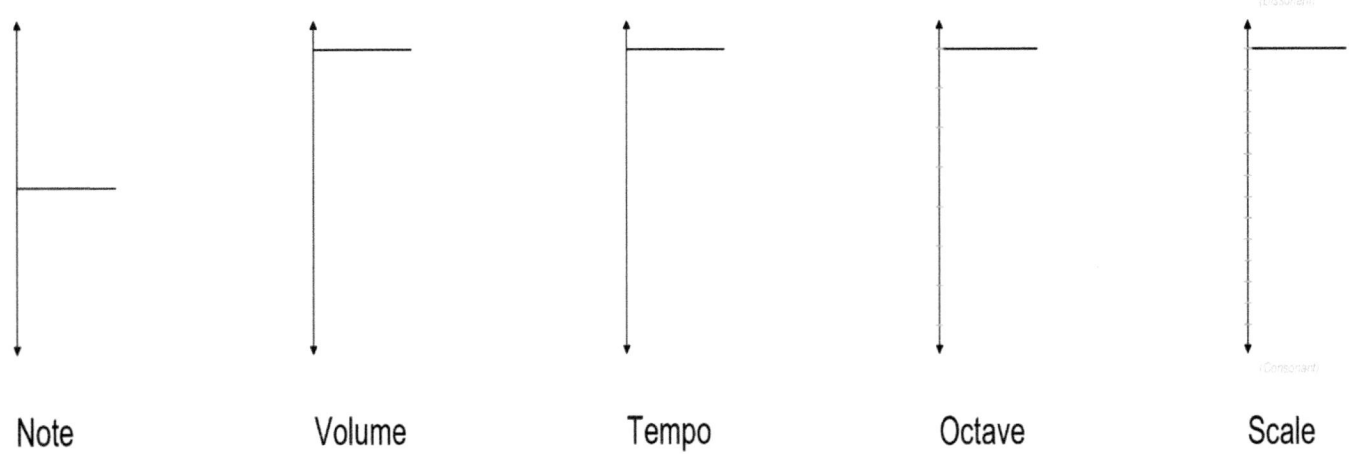

We see that both compositions are going to use the same note.

- The first composition has a very low volume, a very slow tempo, uses the first octave and a consonant scale.
- The second composition has a very high volume, an extremely fast tempo, uses the last octave and a dissonant scale.

It should be clear that these are two completely different pieces of music. They are different for one reason and one reason only: *Music is the interplay of consonance and dissonance on every level.*

Each composition 'interplays' with the music elements differently, and therefore each composition evokes a different feeling, mood, or emotion.

Despite adding more music elements, the **questions** we asked earlier are still relevant.

- Which composition would you choose to fall asleep or relax to?
- Which composition would you choose to get energized?

Do you see that both compositions could be perceived as either consonant or dissonant depending on the Context?

-If you were trying to relax, the first composition would be perceived as consonant.

-If you wanted to be energized, the first composition would be perceived as dissonant.

And vice versa.

Excellent work!

Please, *review this section and make sure everything is clear before you continue.*

SECTION 6—

Let's use our knowledge of Intervals and Scales to build Melodies-

More often than not, melody is thought of as the singer's voice, the lyrics, or the part of the song that we remember or hum. That is true but not all songs have lyrics. So, melody is best thought of as a sequence of intervals that we perceive as a single entity meant to evoke a range of feeling, mood, or emotion.

Note: A melody can be a short sequence of intervals, or a long sequence of intervals. No matter the length of the melody, the goal is the same- to evoke a feeling, mood or emotion.

Fun Fact:

The worlds shortest melody, according to Guinness records is Napalm Death's – **You Suffer**. The entire melody takes 1.3 seconds to play.

The world's longest melody, according to Guinness records is Earthena's- **Symphony of the Crown**. The entire melody takes 48 hours, 39 minutes, and 35 seconds to play.

Though there are no right or wrong ways to construct a melody there is an important guideline that musicians follow.

Let's look at the guideline, then explore how melodies are constructed-

When a musician decides the overall feeling, mood, or emotion they want to convey in their composition, they pick an appropriate scale. For example, if a composer wants to create a song that evokes a relaxing mood, the composer will pick a scale that evokes that mood (i.e., the Major Pentatonic). So, when a composer picks a scale, they do so because the intervals in it create the feeling, mood, or emotion of that specific scale.

Therefore, the sequence of intervals (the melody) needs to include at least some of the 'defining' intervals. If the melody does not include some of the 'defining' intervals the melody will not evoke the feeling, mood, or emotion of that specific scale. (Defeating the purpose of using that scale.)

Let me explain 'defining' intervals-

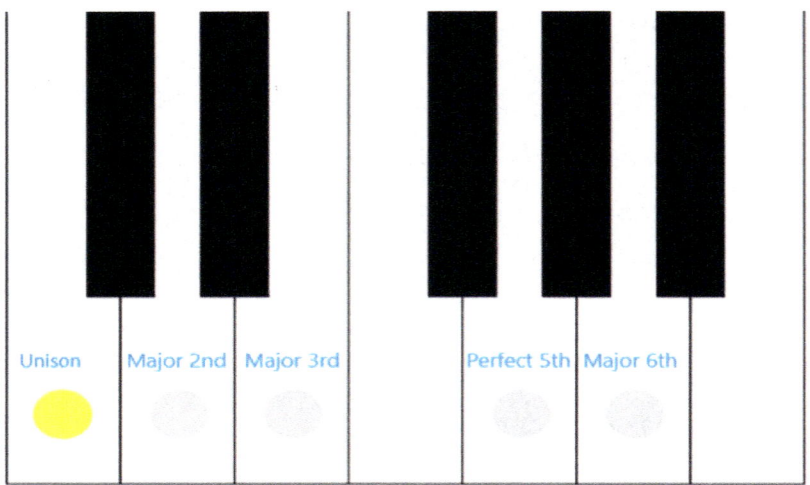

The Major Pentatonic Scale (above) gets its pleasing, consonant sound because it consists of 5 of the most consonant intervals. If you play, for example, a melody that only used the Unison Interval you would not create the overall feeling, mood or emotion of the scale.

Above is a sequence of 4 Unison Intervals. Please play.

Did the melody evoke the feeling, mood or emotion of the Major Pentatonic Scale?

Correct!

This melody did not evoke the mood of the scale because it did not use defining intervals.

Let's look at another example:

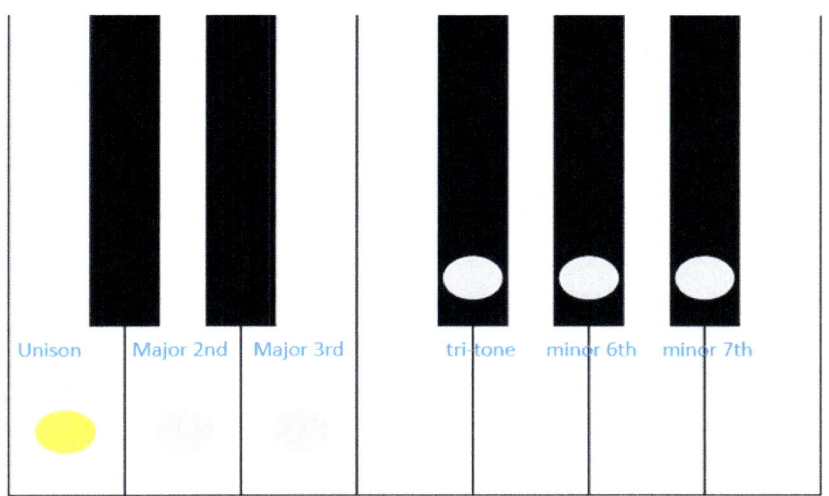

The 'Ambiguous' Scale (above) gets it ambiguous sound because it consists of 3 consonant intervals and 3 dissonant intervals. If you played a melody that only used the consonant intervals, or only the dissonant intervals you would not create the overall feeling mood or emotion of the scale. Defeating the purpose of picking this scale. Try it.

Please, play only the Unison and Major intervals. Did it evoke the mood of the scale?

Correct!

What defines this scale is the combination of consonant and dissonant intervals. In order to evoke the mood of this scale, you would need to play a melody that consisted of at least one consonant and one dissonant interval.

Try it out.

Please, play one consonant interval followed by one dissonant interval or vice versa.

Do you clearly see that by playing the defining intervals you were able to evoke the mood of the scale?

Great!

Note: *understanding the defining intervals of any scale will prove to have great advantages in your learning, and playing. It will not only help you learn scales faster but it will increase your overall connection and appreciation for music.*

How melodies are constructed:

It's important to understand that-

- There are no right or wrong melodies- (any sequence of intervals that evokes a feeling, mood, or emotion is a valid melody)
- There is an infinite number of ways to sequence intervals- (therefore there is an infinite number of possible melodies)
- Inspiration for a melody can come from anywhere- some songs might use the lyrics of a Hymn, some songs might use a Folk Tale, and some might use an Experience (e.g., what does it feel like to 'Love' someone or something)

No matter where inspiration comes from, the goal of every melody is the same; to communicate a story, share life lessons. To evoke a range of feeling, moods, and emotions, expressing what it means to be human.

Fun Fact:

It has been rumored that Beethoven once mimicked the sound of his indigestion to create a melody.

Similar to how a written story (i.e., a book) can be viewed as a single entity, but in actuality it is comprised of several smaller units (i.e., words, sentence's, paragraphs, chapters), melodies are comprised of several smaller units. (i.e., motifs, phrases, sections-etc.).

<u>A motif is the smallest unit that contains thematic material.</u> Its best to think of a motif as a small, complete musical idea-*like a word-* (We will look at some examples in a moment.)

When we combine multiple motifs together, we create a musical phrase-*like a sentence*

When we combine multiple phrases together, we create a section - *like a paragraph-* *(you might have heard of verse and chorus).*

When we combine multiple sections together, we create a song- *like a story*

When we combine multiple songs together, we create an album- *like a story series- (like the Harry Potter Series).*

Using the Major Pentatonic Scale, (but any scale will do) let's create and compare the overall feeling, mood or emotion of 3 different motifs-

Each motif, for this demonstration, will be a sequence of 4 intervals. But like we said, it could be any length.

Just a couple of things before we begin: The images below are not traditional music notation. It will serve our needs until we learn how to read and write music. When you're asked to play an example please start from the top and work your way downward (This will make sense in a moment). Furthermore, throughout this course you have been playing in what is called Free-Time. Free-Time implies that the musician is free to decide how long to play each note and how much silence there is between notes. Free-Time is one of the two main rhythmic categories. We will cover both later. For all of these examples continue to play in Free-Time. As you play, stay relaxed and breathe calmly. Take notice that each time you repeat the melody you use less energy to find the notes.

Motif 1 –

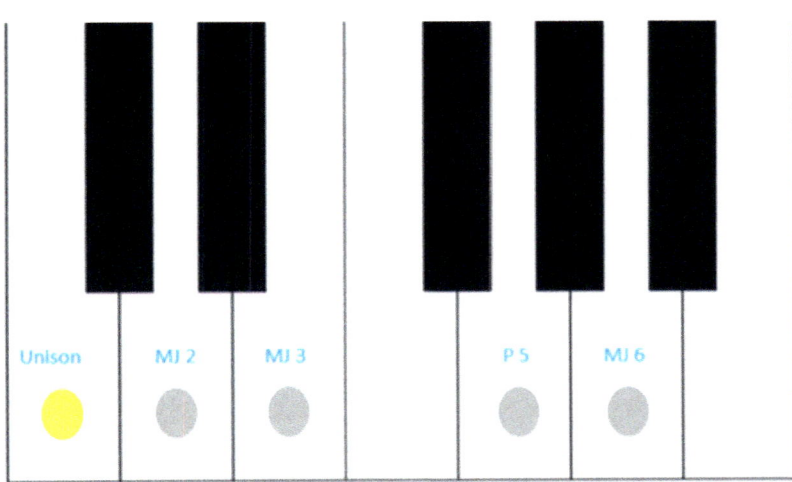

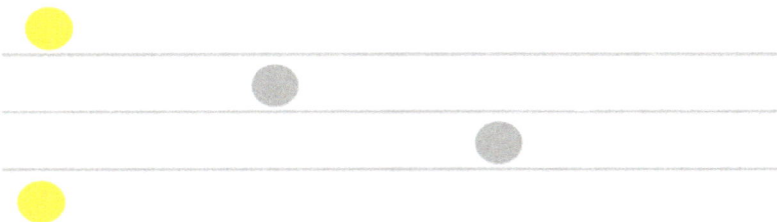

Above is our first example of a motif. It consists of a sequence of intervals that starts on the Tonal Center, then goes to the Major 3rd, the Perfect 5th and then back to the Tonal Center.

Please, play the motif a couple of times, or until you can find the notes easily. Think about the overall feeling, mood or emotion of the motif as we will compare it to the next two motifs. Don't forget to experiment with the pedal as well as varying the volume. Feel free to play the motif in multiple Octaves.

Motif 2

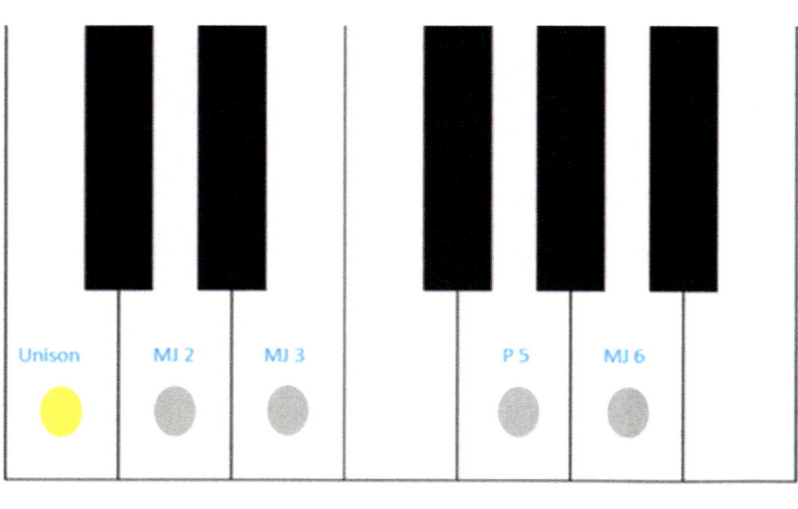

The above motif consists of a sequence of intervals that starts on the Tonal Center, then goes to the Major 6th, the Major 2nd and then back to the Tonal Center. This motif is a sequence of slightly less consonant intervals than the first motif. Therefore, it should sound slightly less consonant.

Please, play the motif a couple of times, or until you can find the notes easily. Think about the overall feeling, mood or emotion of the motif. Don't forget to experiment with the pedal as well as varying the volume. Feel free to play the motif in multiple Octaves.

Did this motif evoke a different feeling or mood than the first motif?

Correct!

This motif evoked a different feeling, mood, or emotion than the first motif because it is a different sequence of intervals.

Motif 3

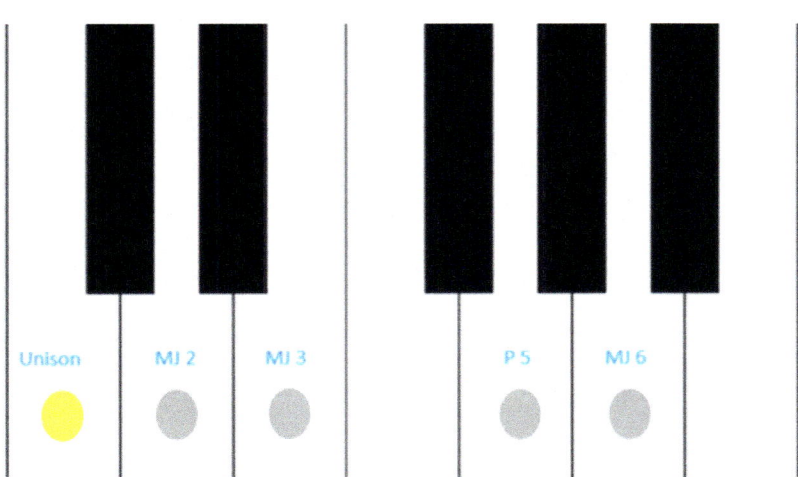

Above is our third example of a 4-note motif. It consists of a sequence of Unison intervals.

Please, play the motif. Think about the overall feeling, mood or emotion. Don't forget to experiment with the pedal as well as varying the volume. Feel free to play the motif in multiple Octaves.

Did this motif evoke a different feeling, or mood than the other motifs?

Yes, you are right!

This motif did evoke a different feeling, but this motif did not use any defining intervals, therefore the feeling, mood or emotion of this scale was not defined. As you will see in a moment, we can combine this motif with a motif that does contain defining intervals to make a musical phrase.

Please, play all three motifs back-to-back. As you do, notice that each motif was built from the same scale but used a different sequence of intervals to create a slightly different feeling, mood or emotion.

Great work!

This is where the fun really begins- at this point we cannot do anything wrong- there are no 'wrong' melodies.

Let's recap-

- Each motif can be viewed as a melodic unit (a mini-melody), whereas each unit is a sequence of intervals that can evoke a range of feelings, moods, and emotions
- A melody can consist of any number of melodic units

Therefore, we could use one motif as the melody. It would be a short melody but it will still evoke a feeling, mood, or emotion.

There are a multitude of other possibilities-

We could combine motifs (melodic units) in multiple ways to create bigger units; like phrases, sections or songs.

Let's combine our 3 motifs, in various ways, to create Melodic Phrases-

For example, we could combine motif-

1 and 2 to create a melodic phrase or,

2 and 1 to create a different melodic phrase or,

We could combine all 3 motifs, 1 and 3 and 2 to create a different melodic phrase... etc.

There are more ways to vary these three motifs, but this is enough for you to understand the overall concept.

Let's combine motif 1 and 2 to create an 8 note melodic phrase (A musical sentence)-

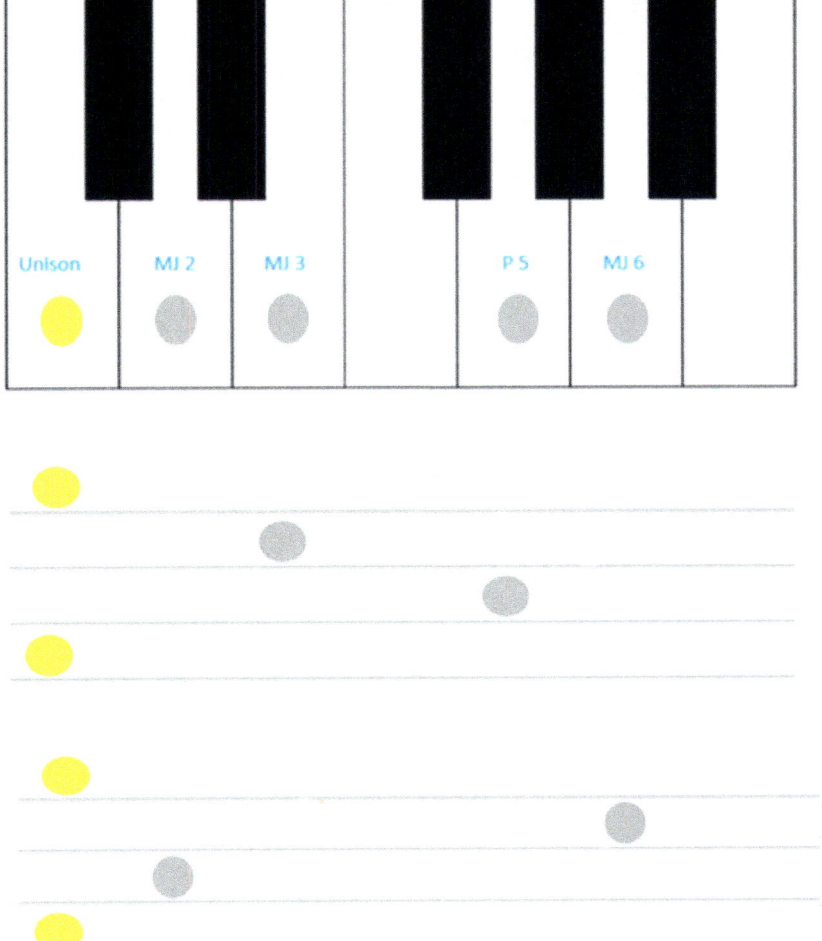

Above is 8-note **melodic phrase** (It consists of two motifs).

Please, play the music phrase a couple of times, or until you can find the notes easily. Think about the overall feeling, mood or emotion of the melodic phrase. Don't forget to experiment with the pedal as well as varying the volume. Feel free to play the melodic phrase in multiple Octaves.

Now, for comparison let's combine motif 2 and 1 to create another 8 note melodic phrase-

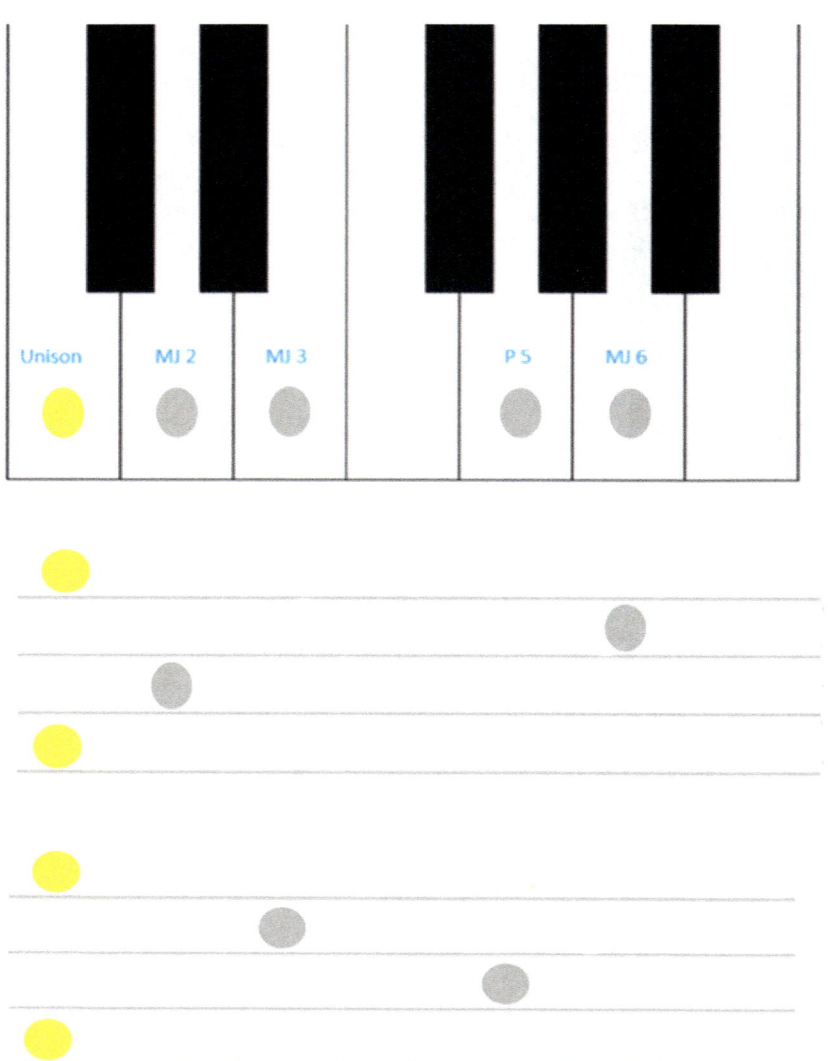

Above is our second 8-note melodic phrase. (It also consists of two motifs.)

Please, play the melodic phrase a couple of times, or until you can find the notes easily. Think about the overall feeling, mood or emotion of the melodic phrase. Don't forget to experiment with the pedal as well as varying the volume. Feel free to play the melodic phrase in multiple Octaves.

Do you agree that this phrase evoked a different feeling, mood, or emotion than the first phrase?

Great!

This phrase was a different sequence of intervals, thus evoking a different feeling, mood, or emotion.

Let's, combine motif 1, 3, 2 and 3 to create a 16-note melodic phrase-

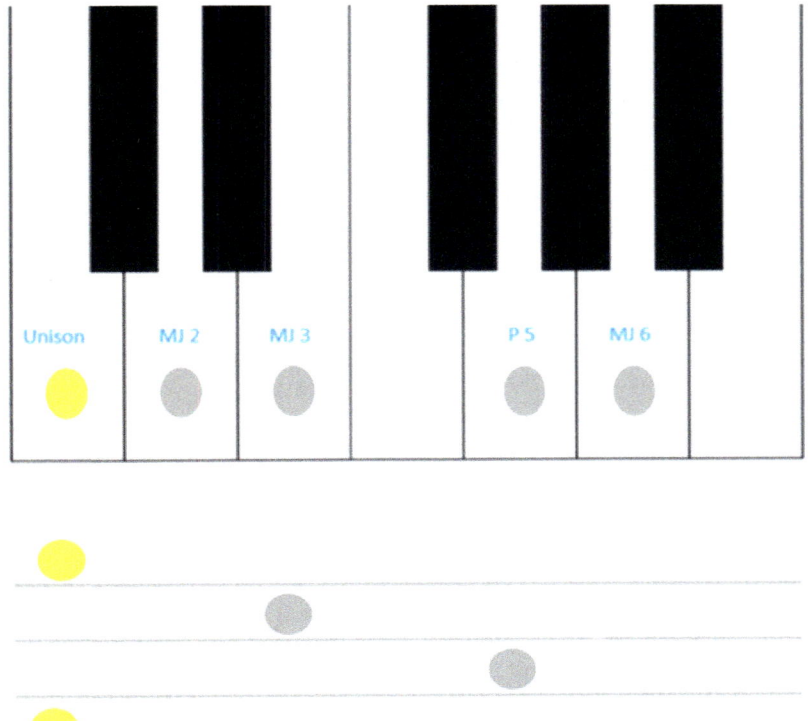

Above is a 16-note phrase. (It consists of four, 4-note motifs.)

Please, play the melodic phrase a couple of times, or until you can find the notes easily. Think about the overall feeling, mood or emotion of the melodic phrase. Don't forget to experiment with the pedal as well as varying the volume. Feel free to play the melodic phrase in multiple Octaves.

I think you're beginning to see that the possibilities are endless. A melody can be a single motif or can combine with other motifs to create musical phrases. Musical phrases can combine to create sections (i.e., like a chorus or a verse). And sections can combine to create an entire song. This is the blueprint that musicians have used throughout history and will continue using to create all the melodies you will ever encounter.

Great work!

Bonus:

A brief, but solid introduction to Rhythm-

Without even paying attention to it, everything you have played throughout this course was rhythmic. This is mainly due to the fact that rhythm is part of our inherent nature. From our beating hearts to pounding waves we cannot escape rhythm. Certain rhythms make us dance while other rhythms calm us. Furthermore, each rhythmic variation will evoke a different feeling, mood, or emotion. As we will see in upcoming examples.

But what exactly is Rhythm?

Let's begin with the 'text book' definition: rhythm is the arrangement of musical sounds according to duration, periodic stress and silence.

In my opinion the definition falls short. More accurately, rhythm is the _physical effect_ we experience as a result of _hearing_ an arrangement of musical sounds according to duration, silence, and periodic stress.

Note:

- *Duration refers to how long a particular sound is played-(i.e., was the note played for 1 second or 100 seconds?)*
- *Silence refers to the absence of sound- (the time in-between the sounds)*
- *Periodic Stress refers to the note or notes that were played slightly louder (accentuating or highlighting them)*

There are two main categories of rhythm, **Free-Time** and **Metered-Time.**

Free-Time is easy to comprehend. It implies that the musician is 'Free' to decide how long to play each note, how much silence there is in-between the notes, and which notes to accentuate. Similar to how we speak.

However, **Metered-Time** is more structured. Generally speaking, Metered-Time is music that is played with respect and consideration to a meter or time piece. Think metronome or the ticking of a clock.

Metered-Time is easier to comprehend if you're given an example-

Let's play a melody using both rhythmic styles and compare- We will first play in Free-Time then Metered-Time.

Free-Time- This is a 4-note melody but any length melody will do.

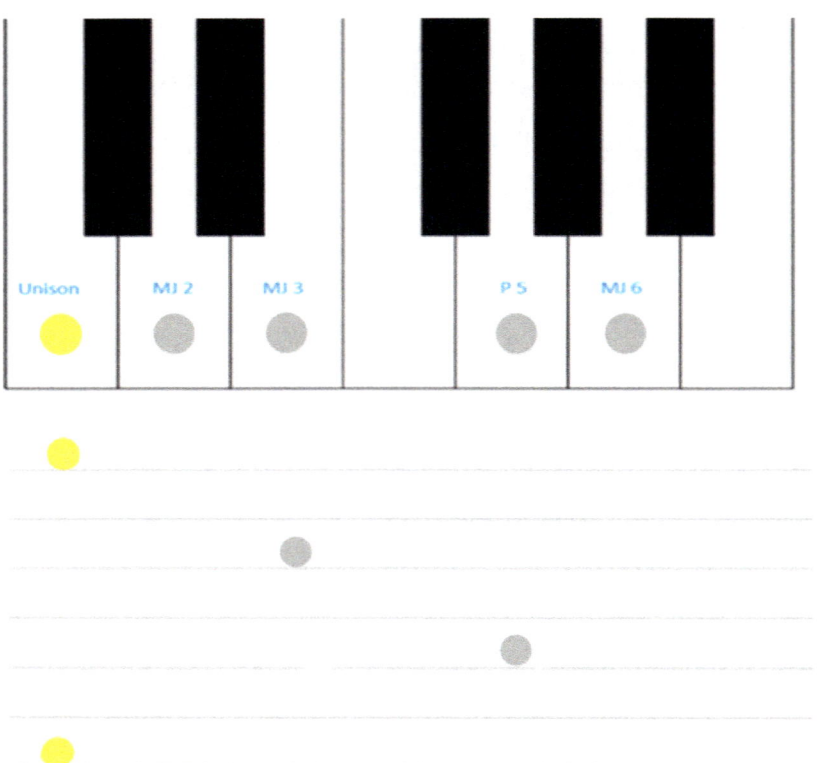

Please, play this melody in the same manner as you have throughout this course- play each note as long as you like, leave as much silence in-between the notes, and accentuate any note or notes you wish. Don't forget to experiment with the pedal as well as varying the volume. Feel free to play the motif in multiple Octaves.

Now, let's play the same melody in Metered-Time- *Instructions on how to do this are below*

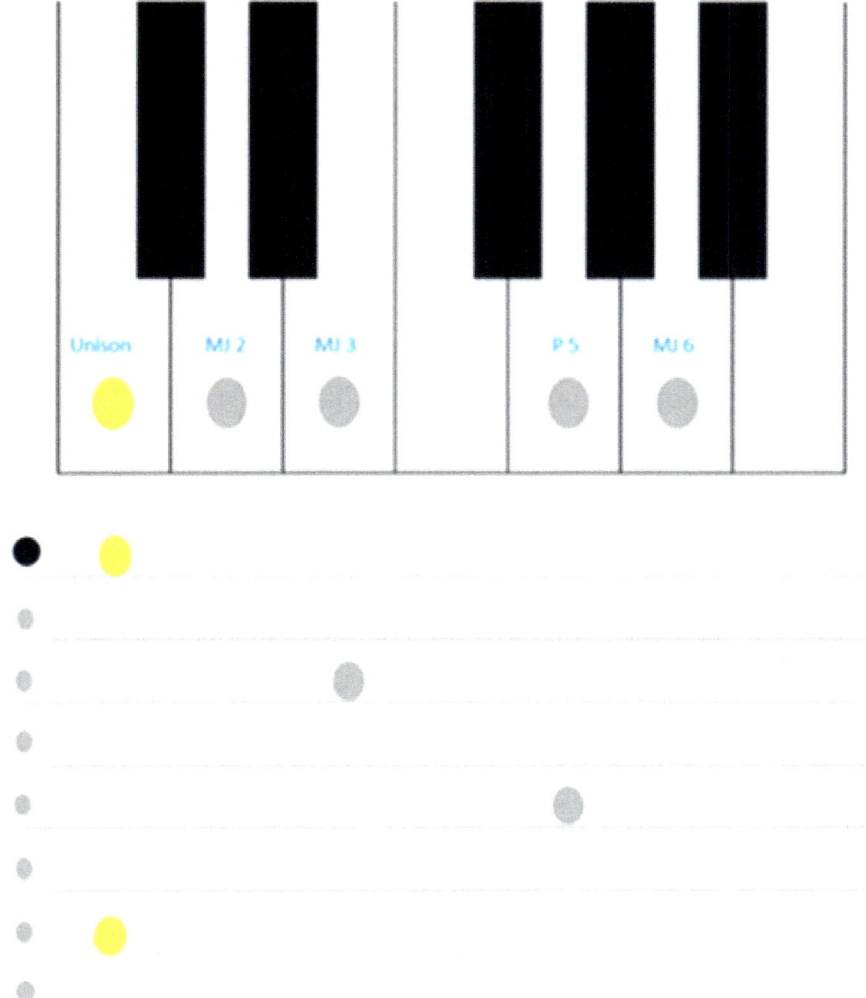

Instructions-

The column of black and grey dots, on the left, represents the 'tics' of a clock-whereas each dot represents one second. The black note indicates the accentuated note. Play this note slightly louder than the others.

If you do not have a clock or a metronome that is no problem. Simply count out loud, as accurately as possible, **1**, 2, 3, 4, 5, 6, 7, 8 and then repeat **1**, 2, 3....

It might help you if you nod your head and/or tap your foot as you count.

When you're comfortable, **please play** each note with the appropriate 'tic'. Don't forget to accentuate the note on the black dot.

Please, repeat a couple of times until playing and counting becomes easy.

Note: playing and counting at the same time, is most likely new to you. It might not be easy at first but after a couple of times you will get it. Take a breath and relax-you are only a few moments away from doing it with ease. Lastly, remember to experiment with the pedal as well as varying the volume. Feel free to play the melody in multiple Octaves.

Question:

Do you agree that the melody evoked, different feeling, mood, or emotion than it did in Free-Time?

Great!

By changing the rhythm, we were able to evoke a slightly different feeling, mood, and emotion.

Now, let's play it again- This time we are going to make a change to the note that gets accentuated. This small variation is enough to change the rhythm.

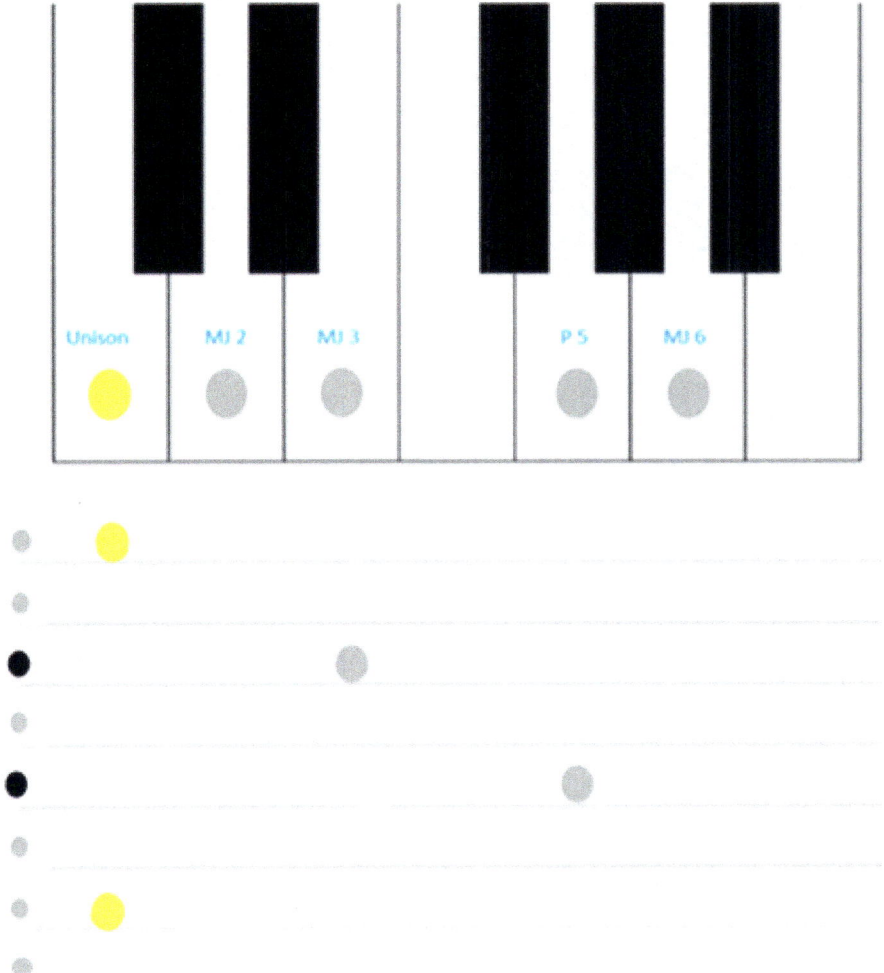

Again, as accurately as possible, count out loud- 1, 2, **3**, 4, **5**, 6, 7, 8 and then repeat 1, 2, **3**....

It might help you to nod your head and/or tap your foot as you count out loud.

When you're comfortable, **please play** each note with the appropriate 'tic'. Don't forget to accentuate the note on the black dot.

Please, repeat a couple of times until this becomes easy. Don't forget to experiment with the pedal as well as varying the volume. Feel free to play the melody in multiple Octaves.

Do you agree that this version sounded and evoked a different feeling, mood, or emotion than the two previous examples?

One last example-This time we are going change when the notes get played. Notice that the third note has moved up one 'tic' or one second.

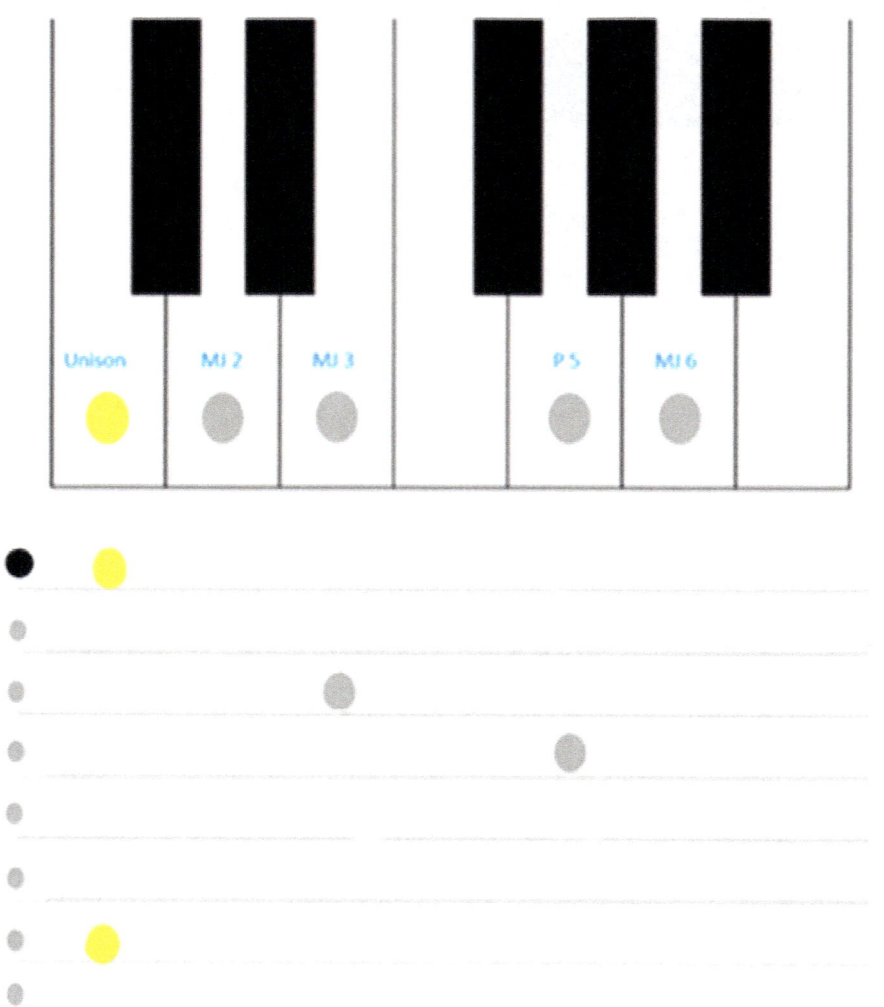

Again, as accurately as possible, count out loud- **1**, 2, 3, 4, 5, 6, 7, 8 and then repeat **1,** 2, 3.... It might help you to nod your head and/or tap your foot as you count out loud.

When you're comfortable, **please play** each note with the appropriate 'tic'. Don't forget to accentuate the note on the black dot.

Please, repeat a couple of times until this becomes easy. Don't forget to experiment with the pedal as well as varying the volume. Feel free to play the melody in multiple Octaves.

Do you agree that this version sounded and evoked a different feeling, mood, or emotion than the three previous examples?

Note: You might have noticed that in our examples we varied Metered-Time in 3 different ways. We played two versions of the melody that accentuated different notes and then we played a version of the melody where the notes were played on different 'tics'. It needs to be stated that there are multiple ways to vary the structure of Metered-Time, each having its own signature sound. Each variation is aptly called a Time Signature. In future lessons, we will learn more about Time Signatures but for now, feel confident that you have a fundamental understanding.

Both rhythmic categories are equally valid, and both are suited for different compositional needs. Think for a moment about a multi-instrument orchestra, if each instrument was playing in Free-Time the orchestra would sound chaotic. The conductor keeps time *(creates a meter)* for the musicians ensuring that all the instruments interweave together seamlessly. If a composer, for example, wanted to create music that evoked- 'The unpredictable sounds heard in a thunderstorm', Free-Time would better suit those compositional needs.

The main take away is that no matter if you are playing in Free-Time or Metered-Time, each variation of rhythm will affect the melody. Each variation will evoke a different feeling, mood, or emotion. Therefore, Rhythm is a Music Element. As we will learn in the History section, certain musical genres are defined by their rhythms. Example: the rhythms in salsa music are completely different than the rhythms in reggae music.

Excellent work!

Please, review this section before you continue and make sure everything is clear.

SECTION 7-

The last Music Element that we will cover in this pre-requisite course is Harmony:

First and foremost, the terms- Harmonize, Harmony, Harmonious, and Harmony Section are often misused leading to unnecessary confusion. (Fair warning- this explanation reads like a tongue twister.) When two notes mix together, they are Harmonizing. The Harmonizing notes create a Harmony (i.e., an interval). But not all Harmonies are Harmonious (i.e., consonant harmonies are harmonious whereas dissonant harmonies are discordant). The Harmony Section refers to note or notes that Harmonize with the melody; the intent is to embellish, support or accompany it.

Let's use a relatable analogy to help us understand what a Harmony Section is and does? -

If we think of the melody as the 'singer', then it's fair to think of the Harmony Section as the 'back-up singer' or 'singers'. Again, the main intention or goal of the Harmony Section, whether it is one back-up singer or multiple singers is always the same: accompany, enrich and support the melody.

Furthermore, no matter the size *(one back-up singer or multiple back-up singers)* the main challenge is always the same- *control the levels of consonance and dissonance between the melody and the harmony section.*

The good news is that you already know to how to do this.

Let me illustrate-

For this example, let's use a very simple melody. The Tonal Center is 261 but any Tonal Center will do.

Using what you know, answer this question-

If our harmony section consisted of one back-up singer, what interval would you ask (him or her) to sing in order to create a <u>consonant harmony</u> for this melody?

Remember: generally speaking, Unison through Major 2nd are consonant. Major 7th through tri-tone are dissonant. Furthermore, Unison is the most consonant interval and the tri-tone is the most dissonant.

Correct-

The back-up singer could sing the same note as the melody *(creating a Unison interval)*.

Note: *As a rule of thumb, the notes of the harmony section are played with a slightly lower volume and in a lower octave then the melody.*

Please, using your index finger from your right hand **play** the yellow dot. Using your index finger from your left-hand **play** any of the grey dots either separately or any two together. If you want to play two grey dots together, I suggest using your pinky and thumb from your left hand. As you're experimenting it is important to think about the fact that you are embellishing the melody.

Furthermore, we can expand our answer to include any of the consonant intervals *(i.e., Unison through Major 2$^{nd})$*.

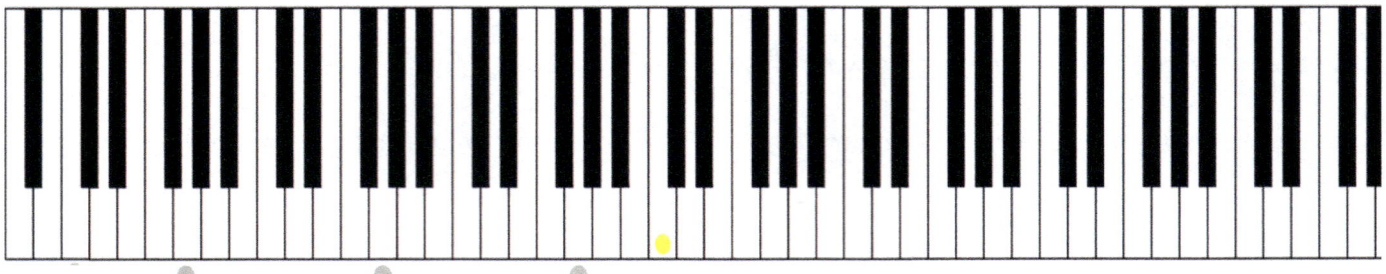

For example, let's harmonize the melody note using the Perfect 5th. Remember-to create a perfect 5th you either go up 7 half-steps or down 5 half-steps.

Please, using your index finger from your left-hand **play** any of the grey dots either separately or any two together. If you want to play two grey dots together, I suggest using your pinky and thumb from your left hand. As you're experimenting it is important to think about the fact that you are embellishing the melody.

Now, if we wanted the Harmony Section to create a dissonant harmony with the melody, what interval or intervals do you think could be sung? *Remember that generally speaking, Unison through Major 2nd are consonant. Major 7th through tri-tone are dissonant.*

Correct!

The harmony section could sing any of the dissonant intervals.

Please, using your index finger from your left-hand **play** any of the grey dots either separately or any two together. If you want to play two grey dots together, I suggest using your pinky and thumb from your left hand. As you're experimenting it is important to think about the fact that you are embellishing the melody.

Next, please pick any other dissonant interval and harmonize it with the melody. If you don't remember all or the intervals and how to create them, please refer to your chart.

Let's recap:

By simply adding a harmony section we can enrich any melody. By varying the interval between the harmony and melody we can vary the amount of consonance and dissonance there is.

Now this is where it gets even more interesting…and fun!

Let's expand on the harmony section and add more 'back-up' singers. For this example, we will have a total of 3 singers. Let's have them all sing different notes.

The music term used to describe two or more notes that come together to embellish a melody is called a Chord- it might be easy to think of a Chord the same way that you think of a Chorus.

The goal and the challenges are the same- accompany, embellish and enrich the melody whilst controlling the levels of consonance and dissonance between the melody and the harmony section.

At first this might seem harder but in actuality, it works the same way as if there was one back-up singer.

What you need to realize is that no matter how many back-up singers there are (how big the chord is) each back-up singer is mixing with the melody and is creating an interval. If there are 3 back-up singers then there are 3 intervals.

So, for example, if all 3 back-up singers are all singing consonant intervals, then the harmony section will sound consonant.

Let's take a look-

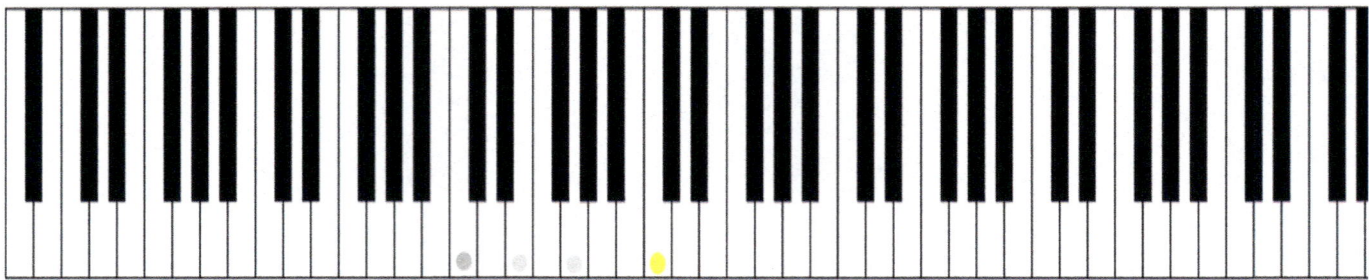

In the above example, we see that there are 3 back-up singers- each one is singing a consonant interval. Starting from the left- an Octave, a Major 3rd and a Perfect 5th.

Please, play the yellow dot with your index finger from your right hand and play the grey dots with your ring, middle, and thumb from you left hand.

Congratulations! -*You just played your first chord! Furthermore, you played with more than your pointer fingers and you used both hands.*

Excellent progress!

Now let's compare it to a harmony section with all dissonant intervals-

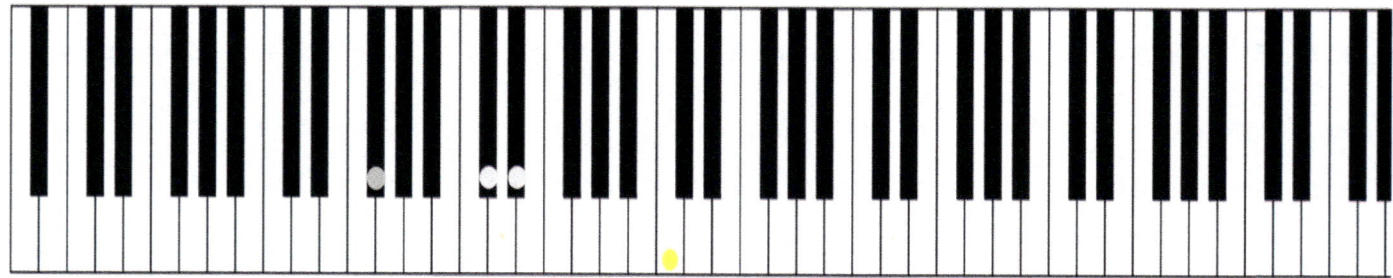

Again, there are 3 back-up singers- but this time, each one is singing a dissonant interval. Starting from the left- a tri-tone, a minor 2nd and a minor 3rd.

This is an extensive and expansive topic that hopefully you will enjoy a lifetime exploring. As you continue to learn more, approach each chord as a chorus or as back-up singers who are embellishing and accompanying the melody. Each chord, or harmony section will evoke a different feeling, mood, or emotion. Therefore, Harmony Sections are a music element.

Great work!

Let's finally answer these questions- If there are an infinite number of frequencies in the universe, why do we only use 12? Why these specific 12?

To help us, let's quickly review our 'real-life' example from the beginning of the course-

- You are peacefully sitting in your home- after some arbitrary amount of time you desire change. As the desire for change builds- tension builds. So, to release the tension, for example, you decide to go out for a walk.

It's fair to say that you were 'Home', then you went 'Away' (Out for a walk).

What we want to realize is that after some arbitrary amount of time being 'Away', you will eventually desire to return 'Home'. As nice as being away is, you're not going to want to stay 'Away' for the rest of your life.

Question-

Have you ever noticed that whenever you are 'Away' and you decide that it's time to go home, anticipation builds?

Furthermore, have you ever noticed that when you're on your way home if you notice something that reminds you or signals to you that your almost home, *like a familiar landmark,* the anticipation elevates even further?

Well, music works the same way.

Let's take a look-

More often than not, a song will start and finish on the Initial note (the Tonal Center). So, we can view the Tonal Center as the 'Home' of the song and we can view the notes of the melody as the 'Away' of the song.

Now, as good as any song might be after some arbitrary amount of time (on average 3 minutes and 30 seconds) we will want the song to come to an end. When we desire the song to end, we don't want it to just stop, we want it to return back 'Home' -to the Tonal Center.

So, when we sense that a song is coming to an end, anticipation builds. Like in our 'real-life' example, when you're on your way home and notice something that reminds you that your almost home, anticipation elevates even further.

In real-life it's easy to think of examples of landmarks, *but a musical landmark might be a little harder to comprehend*?

Let's use the sliding scale of intervals to help us figure out what might be the musical landmark-

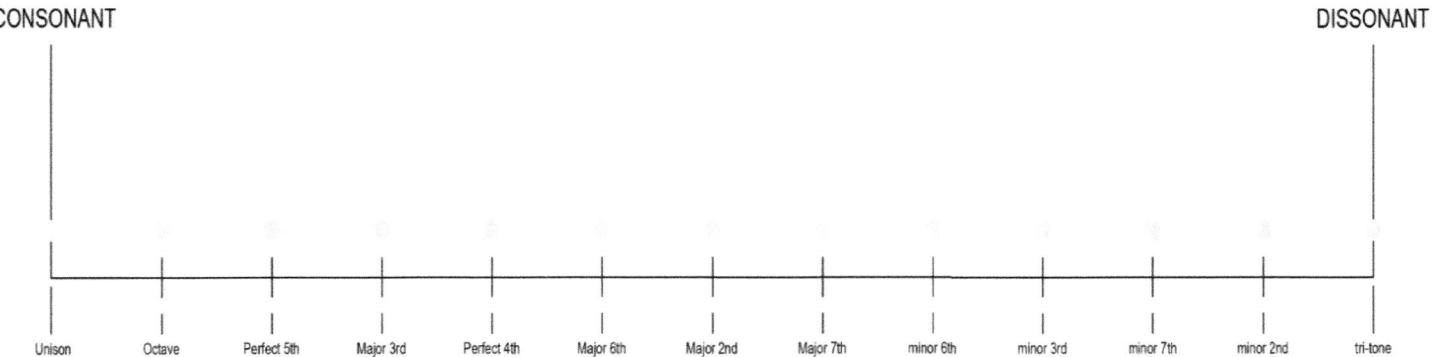

Remember- the yellow dot indicates the Tonal Center

- Each interval is a soundwave merging with the soundwave of the Tonal Center
- The more the two soundwaves have in <u>common</u> the more they merge

When you look at all the intervals on the 'sliding scale' you see that the Octave and the perfect 5th are the closest intervals to the Tonal Center. They have the most in <u>common.</u>

Since we hear the Octave as being 'similar' to the Tonal Center it does not act like a landmark. However, the Perfect 5th, because it has the most in common with the Tonal Center, acts like a 'musical landmark'!

Let's recap:

No matter the song we are listening to, we will eventually want it to end. When we sense that the song is coming to an end, anticipation builds. When we hear the perfect 5th, it signals to us that we are almost home- elevating the anticipation even further.

So, as it turns out, our Music Alphabet is a celebration of the Perfect 5th. It is celebration of the 'musical landmark'.

At first this will be hard to comprehend, but our music alphabet is a series of Perfect 5th's.

Let's me explain-

Let's use 27.5 as our Tonal Center. It has a perfect 5th… Then, if we use the perfect 5th of the Tonal Center as our <u>new</u> Tonal Center, it too will have its own perfect 5th. Then, if we use that perfect 5th as the <u>new</u> Tonal

Center, it will have its own perfect 5th. When we continue to repeat the process, we will get 11 different notes. However, after the 11th note we will hear a sound that we recognize as both different, and similar to our initial Tonal Center of 27.5.

Let me illustrate-

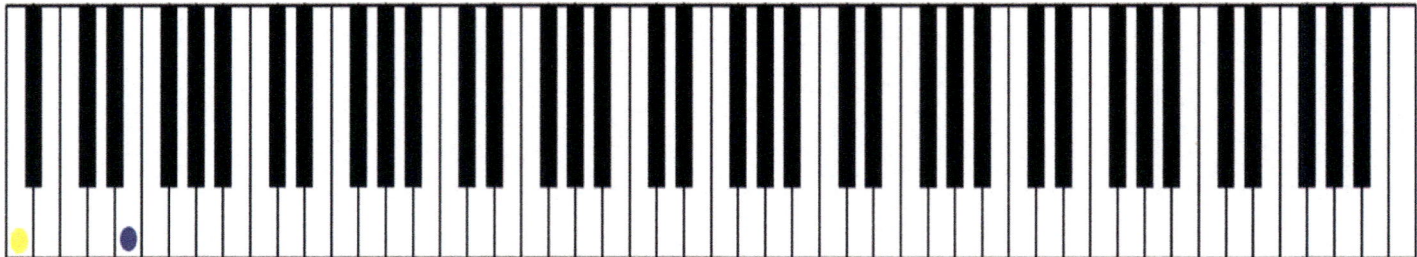

The yellow dot is our Tonal Center (27.5). If we want to locate its perfect 5th, we simply count up 7 half-steps to the blue dot. Now, let's make the perfect 5th (the blue dot) our <u>new</u> Tonal Center…

The yellow dot is our <u>new</u> Tonal Center. If we want to locate its perfect 5th, we simply count up 7 half-steps to the blue dot. Now, let's make the perfect 5th (the blue dot) our <u>new</u> Tonal Center…

The yellow dot is our <u>new</u> Tonal Center. If we want to locate its perfect 5th, we simply count up 7 half-steps to the blue dot. Now, let's make the perfect 5th (the blue dot) our <u>new</u> Tonal Center…

When we continue to repeat this process...

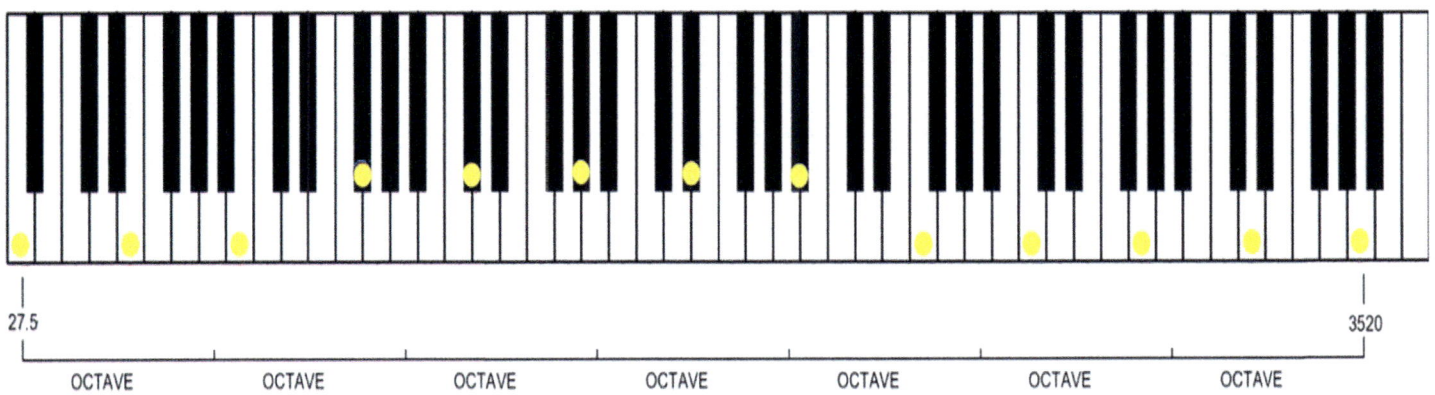

we will end up playing the frequency 3520; which is heard as both different and similar to the original Tonal Center 27.5. 3520 is the frequency of the Tonal Center 7 octaves higher (above diagram). 27.5 and 3520 are in fact different frequencies, and we do hear them as different sounds, but these frequencies are also 'related' to each other. Since they are 'related' we also hear them as similar.

In the series of Perfect 5th's, we will have 11 different new sounds before we hear the similar sound of the initial Tonal Center. It's as if we have ended up where we started, and for this reason we refer to the series of Perfect 5ths as the Circle of Fifths.

When we count all the notes, the 12 notes of our music alphabet are revealed.

Note: *When you were first introduced to the frequencies of the music alphabet, they were presented to you in one octave. Now you are seeing them spread across the entire piano. Since we hear frequencies that are doubled* *or divided as similar, we can divide all the frequencies, as many times as the piano will allow and they will all fit nicely in one octave! The image below should look familiar.*

Congratualtions on completing the pre-requisite course!

As you continue your studies, remember-

Music is the result of organizing sound, in various ways, to express or communicate our story, to share life lessons, to evoke a range of feeling, moods, and emotions- expressing what it means to be human.

In order to do this, we 'Interplay' with Music Elements; whereas each element has a range of choices for us to interplay with. Each interplay, depending on <u>Context</u>, will be perceived as some level of consonance or dissonance- evoking a different feeling, mood, or emotion. *Which is the sole purpose of music.*

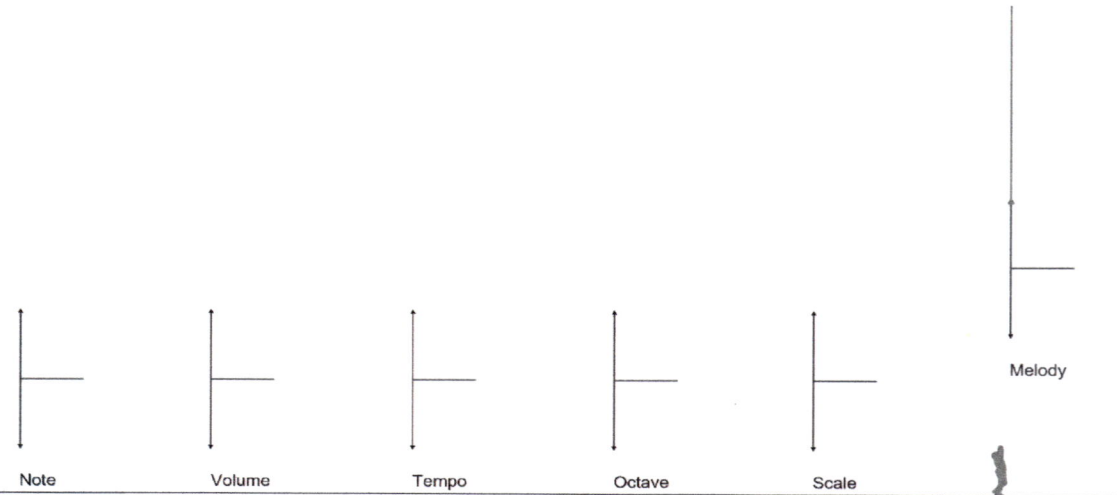

As you continue to learn new elements, simply add them to the music blue print!

Since it might be hard to fully comprehend how much you actually know, and/or know how far ahead of the learning curve you are, we have conducted surveys of students and teachers who have taken, or are teaching, other methodologies; to ask how long it was before they learned or taught the material presented in this pre-requisite course. The answers will absolutley surprise you. The surveys are on the website if you would like to take a look. www.beforeyoulearn.com

Furthermore, if you would like additional help, with any topic, we will be offering Online-Tutoring.

If you would like to be notified when tutoring comes available, visit our website and subscribe.

What's Next:

Here are my suggestions on how to continue: *note: we are currently working on the eBooks for all these topics.*

Learn-

- Note names
- How to read and write sheet music
- Your first songs
- How to practice with purpose- *how to efficeintly practice on, and away from your instrument*
- Posture, breathe and fingering techniques
- More chords, chord progressions, and how to vary
- More scales
- More music elements
- How to improvise and compose-*learn how to use what you already know to create an endless amount of music*
- Song mapping-*in this course you learn to seperate the music elements that are used in any song. For example, you could look at the melody of any song, and map out the melodic units that combine to form the melody. This will help you better understand the construction of any song and help you learn it faster.*

If you would like to be notified when we release the next E-Book, please click on link below and subscribe.

When you subscribe you will receive a coupon code for your next eBook.

www.beforeyoulearn.com

SECTION 8 -

Music History- *A brief, but solid introduction to the evolution of musical genres.*

Note: *As you explore the History Section take note that every genre uses the same music blueprint. The only differnence is that each genre 'interplays' with the music elements differently to suit their compositional needs; to tell the story of their time.*

Welcome to the history section. This section gives you information on the beginning and evolution of music through the ages. An understanding of the When's and How's of musical creation, the understanding of its sociocultural underpinnings and evolution, will give you a more well-rounded knowledge of music. Furthermore, this section will illustrate that music, in all of its evolutionary variations, is fundamentally the same. As you will see, each genre (each evolutionary variation) uses the same musical blueprint but interplays with the music elements differently; evoking a different feeling, mood and emotion.

Let's take a look-

The Greek culture was humanistic; its people leaned away from the church and towards the belief in man's humanity, welfare, values and dignity as its own advancement. The music of the early Greeks was also humanistic. Aristotle believed that a person who listens to the wrong kind of music will grow up wrong, but that the right kind of music would help educate the young. Music was not just sounds for pointless pleasure but had educational and celebratory intent, and could actually affect your character. Music, to the Greeks, had expressive force and could change hearts and improve human nature. Music was about the pursuit of truth and beauty. The Greeks held to the doctrine of Ethos which ascribed to music healing and educative powers. During performance, the early Greeks combined words, music, and movement, reciting poetry over melody as the audience danced. This was a shared and moving experience. Some scholars consider this combination of words and music the first opera.

The Greeks had a special scale for every occasion and you have actually learned some of these

Ionian (this is the Major scale)

Dorian

Phrygian

Lydian

Mixolydian

Aeolian (this is the Natural Minor scale)

Locrian

An example of Greek song is the skolion, a banquet song or drinking song. These heroic tales often reminded the listener to enjoy life.

Here is an example of a skolion called Seikilos Epitaph or Song of Seikilos

Ὅσον ζῇς φαίνου,

Hoson zēs phainou,

While you live, shine,

μηδὲν ὅλως σὺ λυποῦ· mēden holōs sy

lypou;

have no grief at all;

πρὸς ὀλίγον ἐστὶ τὸ ζῆν, pros oligon esti to

zēn,

life exists only for a short while,

τὸ τέλος ὁ χρόνος ἀπαιτεῖ. to telos ho

chronos apaitei. and time demands its toll.

By 146 BCE, Greece had become a Roman state. The powerful empire adopted most of the Greek ideals of music and continued their practice. In a last-ditch effort to unite their empire, the Romans adopted Christianity as their official religion but the once powerful empire still fell in 450 BCE. All collected knowledge, including that musical history, was lost.

We now enter the Middle Ages, or Medieval time, 600-1000 CE known as the Dark Ages, and 1000-1400 CE as the High Middle Ages.

Education and technology, as it was, remained lost; these were truly dark times. As the world was falling apart, the Church stepped forward to preserve what culture was left.

Music changed with the time. The Greek and Roman ideal of humanistic music was replaced. Through the Church, music came to serve one purpose: to evoke the divine beauty of God. Music was played to serve the Church and teach Christian thought. If music extolled the virtues of man, it was rejected as self-centered. Music was no longer celebratory; the dancing and festivals of Ancient Rome were denounced as pagan. All instruments were disallowed. The voice was the sole sound of Christian music and the plainchant its vehicle. There was no beat so there was nothing to dance to. [Highly meditative music]. Dissonance was frowned upon and the tri-tone was forbidden as the devil's interval. This was the age of theocracy and liturgical music.

This was purposeful, in order to create long meditative moods in which the listeners could contemplate God. The Church endeavored to use this liturgical music to re-civilize its troubled constituents.

Music example: Kyrie Eleison

"Lord, have mercy"

You should be recognizing now that music is a product of its time, whether referential or reactive. That the fundamental purpose of music hasn't changed. (To share our story, to evoke feeling, mood and emotion; expressing what it means to be human.)

The music of the Dark Ages was used by the Church essentially as means for social reform, and so was serene and conducive to prayer. As it moves into the High Middle Ages, Europe starts to regain its knowledge and strength. Farming techniques were rediscovered and food production grew. Horses were brought in to take over for the slower ox. Innovations in crop rotation and irrigation lead to more crops and more food, which lead to population growth, which lead to the need for space. Education improved, and cities are built. And music began to evolve and depart from liturgy and service of the Church. Secular music for non-religious use rose in popularity. Pulse returned to music; there was once again a danceable beat. There were new rhythmic systems. Keyboard instruments were born!

The Church was still a presence in those times so the new composers did not completely stray from the plainchant but embellished it.

Music notation was developed out of necessity. Composers were, for the first time, signing and taking ownership of their work; the self was returning to music.

This departure from purely liturgical music was called Organum. It peaked between 1150 and 1300 CE with its star composer, Leonin.

Brief review-

Greece had a humanistic view towards music; life was celebrated through song, dance, and poems via instruments and the human voice.

Greece became a Roman state and Rome made Christianity its official religion but then fell to German invasion. The Pope's power increased and the age of theocracy began with its aim to save humanity from ruin.

The focus of music shifted from humanism and dancing and singing, to meditative music that reminds the listener of God's divinity. The age of liturgical music lasted for about 600 years.

By 1400CE, the church lost its absolute power. Theocracy weakened and secular rulers rose. (Again, every genre uses the same blueprint, the variation comes from the interplay of the music elements that are used.)

We enter the Renaissance!

Renaissance means rebirth; a rebirth of man, the rebirth of humanism.

The focus returned to the exploration and celebration of humanity. Humanity's urge for expression, which had been stifled for centuries by the church, was released with wild abandon. All of the arts began to flourish.

This was an age of exploration, both in the world and within the self.

The Renaissance musicians were trying to recapture the musical ideals of the ancient Greeks and recreate the music of this early history. They grabbed on to the idea of Ethos but realized that the music they were making did not have the restorative and educative affects that they expected; it was too disordered and complex. The Renaissance musicians realized their music needed order in its complexity and created homophony (think one singer and a harmony section) and harmony. The rules of harmony allowed for greater control of the interaction of voices. Some composers of the time were Tallis and Monteverdi.

From 1590-1604, musicians and intellectuals gathered to discuss and experiment with music drama and Opera is born.

In the early 1600s, the focus on vocal music began to shift back to instrumental music, and the Baroque period (1600-1750CE) began.

You will recognize the foremost composers of the time, Bach and Handel.

Their music is polyphonic (think two melodies playing simultaneously). With the creation of harmony and its inherent control, these great composers (Bach, in particular) were able to construct elaborate multi-voiced compositions. [Counterpoint]

The Church, still weak, continued its mission to educate Europe in the word of God. Recognizing the music's complexity, composers' control over harmony and their ability to create music with multiple voices as divine, the Church employed composers to create their music in the service of God.

The composers were utilizing the technique of Counterpoint to create elaborate compositions. Counterpoint, or contrapuntal, means "note against note," and features musicians using their right and left hands concurrently to play separate and distinct melodies. This music was created on the harpsichord and the clavichord. The piano was not yet invented.

Music was motoric, paying strict attention to time, so that multiple voices could successfully interact.

Some popular musical forms were binary, ternary, fugues and inventions. (You will learn these forms in a later course but each of these forms follow the same rules that you learned in the melody section.)

Next comes the classical period from 1750-1825CE.

The musical style of this period mimicked the Greek ideas of Classical art; a celebration of form, and understated and uncluttered symmetry. The melodies echoed the human voice. Classical music was geared towards the middle class. The members of this stratum were hard-working and desired easy melodies to which they could relax after a long day.

Classical music had a steady beat and pulse, with gradual volume change.

Balance, order, and Symmetry were its number one concerns.

Some popular musical forms were the sonata, sonatina, minuet and trio, and theme and variation. (Again, these forms follow the same rules that you learned in the melody section.)

Music was decorated with trills, and crescendo and de-crescendo were the dynamics of choice. (You will learn more about this in another course but all or these decorations are to be viewed as a way to accentuate a note as you learned in the rhythm section.)

Chords were sometimes played in block form but Alberti base was also popular. (You will learn more about how to vary the ways you play chords but for now just remember that chords are like a chorus…and that there are many ways to vary how you play them.)

The composers Hayden and Mozart composed for this audience.

Classical music was essentially a decorative art; pretty and something you kept on in the background to relax. As Europe began to buckle under royal rule and moved towards revolution, Beethoven moved away from Classical and harnessed music's power to express the turmoil of the time. He pushed against the set forms of Classical restraint and explored the expressive possibilities of music, so that the expressive content became the form.

Romantic music was born of the French Revolution. The years between

1820 and 1900 were a time of revolution not only against the monarchy but also against the structure and formality of earlier Classical periods. Music became personal and the artist inserted himself and his feelings into his compositions. The music was emctional, adventurous and passionate, and often "Dolce," or sweet and gentle.

A lot of Classical music sounded similar though it was created by different composers because the restraining forms denied true expression of the creator's self. The expressive qualities of Romantic music allowed the individual composers' voice and personality to shine through. Listeners were able to discriminate the music of different composers and could, through their compositions, get some sense of their lives and histories. This movement, within Romantic music, was known as Nationalism.

The most recognizable composer of this era is Fredrich Chopin.

Some contemporaries are Mendelsohn, Liszt, Verdi and Schumann.

In roughly 1880 began a shift towards Modernism, a genre of revolt against the emotions and drama of the Romantic period. The world was growing and evolving rapidly and music was moving right along with it, so Modernism is a large umbrella under which several musical movements fall.

Impressionism 1880-1900

Moving away from expression of emotion towards exploring one's atmosphere, this genre generally favored short forms and uncommon scales, as its creators experimented with sound. This movement took place predominantly in France, and its famous composers include Debussy, Ravel and Satie. (The Ambiguous Scale was popular in this genre.)

GERMAN EXPRESSIONISM 1860-1911
With the introduction of Freud's ideas of id, ego, and superego, the

German Expressionists turned inward to explore their own psyches musically. Mahler is a prime example of a composer of this movement.

In America during the early 1900s, music was also taking new form. New sounds were reflective of the rapid advancements of society. There were mass media and appliances, plastics and trains. Freud introduced his theories on the human psyche. Quantum theory and special theory challenged religious belief. The world was moving faster and faster and music acted as a mirror. Music was reflection of its time.

BLUES:

In the early 1900s, blues music developed from African-American spirituals, the often-religious working songs of slaves. Blues music, with its distinct scale and rhythms, was not meant to concentrate on the negativity of life, but as a coping mechanism. The true undertone of the blues is not sadness, but hope!

Here are Charlie Butler and Blind Lemon Jefferson

Jazz, 1900-present

This style grew directly from the blues. Like the blues, jazz often used a swing beat, which is an uneven rhythm and syncopation. Syncopation is a rhythm that accents an off-beat, the notes between the main beat.

This style was based on improvisation. While composers throughout music history have improvised, creating music on the spot, in no genre did musicians accomplish this feat so well as in jazz.

Jazz musicians use harmony in a different way – they extend chords farther than musicians in another genre. Three note triads are used very infrequently; you'll often hear quartal and quintal chords. To create richer and more complex sounds, jazz improvisers play in multiple scales and use multiple key centers.

They made use of the musical elements in very creative ways!

Jazz itself evolved quickly. There are many sub-genres and we will explore them in later classes. For now, check out these guys:

Ellington

Coltrane

Thelonius Monk

Chick Corea

Bill Evans

ROCK/POP, 1950-PRESENT

Led Zeppelin, Jimi Hendrix, the Beatles, Cream, the Who, Pearl Jam, Nirvana, the Stones, Foo Fighters... the list goes on and on

For now, we will group all these bands together with the understanding that this genre was based on youth rebellion.

These songs are short, powerful and range from slow ballads to neck breaking tunes. Loud or soft, the message of rock is clear.

Here are two examples of rock and roll songs that rely heavily on keyboard: Your Time is Gonna Come by Led Zeppelin and Angry Young Man by Billy Joel.

For More information on our teaching methods and courses:

Please Contact Us-

sales@beforeyoulearn.com

info@beforeyoulearn.com

We will respond as promptly as possible.

Appendix:

About the Author and How the Unifying Concept Was Discovered

Hello, my name is Eric Fine.

I began learning music theory and how to play the piano about 15 years ago. Like so many, I struggled. It took me a grueling three years to learn the fundamentals. I almost quit every other week.

I became highly motivated to figure out why learning music theory was so hard for most and why there was an unnecessarily high dropout rate. I felt that this issue is not only problematic for students but also has implications for music teachers and society as a whole.

So, 12 years ago, using my bachelor's in education, I set off on a mission to create a better teaching methodology. My first five attempts failed, but four years ago, I had a breakthrough.

While working on a master's degree in social theory, I used *fractals* to study social systems as a way to predict and change behavior. (The main thing to know about *fractals* is that the seemingly complex system is actually governed by one set of instructions. If you know the underlying set of instructions, then you can comprehend the whole.) I began to wonder whether music was a *fractal*.

As it turns out, music is indeed a *fractal*. All music ever made, or ever will be made, is governed by one set of instructions, or what I call the one Unifying Concept. As this course has shown, all music, including all theory, terms, and topics, can be distilled to this Unifying Concept: "Music is the Interplay of Consonance and Dissonance." No matter what aspect of music we are discussing, it can be discussed in these terms. Therefore, an understanding of the underlying set of instructions is all you need to comprehend the whole.

I hope this pre-requisite course served you well,

Eric Fine.

Printed in Great Britain
by Amazon